Len Sweet knows the power of the phrase, "Once upon a time . . ." When people hear these words they awake from their slumber, come to the edge of their seats, tuck the palms of their hands under their chins, and listen. This book did that for me. I was drawn into the wonderful, unique story of Len's mother and family without the expectation of there being anything in it for me. Boy was I wrong.

**RANDY FRAZEE**
Author of *The Heart of the Story*

Leonard Sweet has long been one of my favorite people, and now I know why. Mabel Boggs Sweet. *Mother Tongue*, a spoken portrait of his mother—a woman of simple faith met with the strength, resiliency, and closeness to nature her mountain upbringing provided—is beautifully written, resounding with love and gratitude.

**LISA SAMSON**
Novelist and artist

If anyone ever wondered about the sacred and sacrificial art of Christian mothering joined with the divine calling to put Christ first in all things, meet Mabel Boggs Sweet. The stark stories of her life as a mother, shunned and poor, are contrasts to her extraordinary ability to live her life all for Christ. Thank you, Len Sweet, for telling us about your mother. She surely did cast a long shadow, and now we can sit in it, be encouraged, and learn.

**MARYKATE MORSE**
Professor of leadership and spiritual formation,
George Fox Evangelical Seminary

A treasure trove of life lessons and secrets that Len's mom left behind for him and his brothers (and now you and me) as a legacy to grow on. Len's sheer brilliance in making applications of the metaphors and meaning behind his mom's legacy in relation to the gospel and the history of the church enables him to seamlessly lace the two together in a rich and luxurious feast at Christ's table. Enjoy the banquet!

**MARK J. CHIRONNA**
Bishop of Church on the Living Edge

Had I known Mabel Boggs Sweet in the flesh, I would have been in awe of her. Even on the page, she stuns me. Gritty and outspoken, she was a gifted preacher and a frustrated feminist. Her favorite teacher was the Bible, and yet she firmly believed everyone had something to teach her. While Jesus was the unchanging center of her life, her faith was strong enough to embrace mystery. A gorgeous tribute to her, *Mother Tongue* is both moving and entertaining. I thoroughly enjoyed it!

**LYNNE HYBELS**
Author of *Nice Girls Don't Change the World*

A treasure of metaphor and story from the voice of a mother who birthed and raised a prolific theologian. You can hear her voice, see her fire, and appreciate the passion and power she had to love boldly and stand in the face of great odds. You will want to sit at the feet of this woman.

**REV. DR. DOTTIE ESCOBEDO-FRANK**
District superintendent, United Methodist Church

HOW OUR
HERITAGE
SHAPES OUR
STORY

*Mother Tongue*

LEONARD
SWEET

A NavPress resource published in alliance
with Tyndale House Publishers, Inc.

NavPress is the publishing ministry of The Navigators, an international Christian organization and leader in personal spiritual development. NavPress is committed to helping people grow spiritually and enjoy lives of meaning and hope through personal and group resources that are biblically rooted, culturally relevant, and highly practical.

**For more information, visit www.NavPress.com.**

*Mother Tongue: How Our Heritage Shapes Our Story*

Copyright © 2017 by Leonard Sweet. All rights reserved.

A NavPress resource published in alliance with Tyndale House Publishers, Inc.

*NAVPRESS* and the NAVPRESS logo are registered trademarks of NavPress, The Navigators, Colorado Springs, CO. *TYNDALE* is a registered trademark of Tyndale House Publishers, Inc. Absence of ® in connection with marks of NavPress or other parties does not indicate an absence of registration of those marks.

Cover photograph of paper texture copyright © darkbird/Adobe Stock. All rights reserved.
Cover illustration of people copyright © majivecka/Adobe Stock. All rights reserved.
Cover photograph of manuscripts copyright © Scisetti Alfio/Adobe Stock. All rights reserved.
Insert photographs are from the personal collection of the author and are used with permission.

The Team:
Don Pape, Publisher
David Zimmerman, Acquisitions Editor
Ron Kaufmann, Designer

Published in association with the literary agency of Mark Sweeney & Associates.

All Scripture quotations, unless otherwise indicated, are taken from the Holy Bible, *New International Version,*® *NIV.*® Copyright © 1973, 1978, 1984, 2011 by Biblica, Inc.® Used by permission. All rights reserved worldwide. Scripture quotations marked DRV are taken from the *Holy Bible*, Douay-Rheims Version, which is in the public domain. Scripture quotations marked ESV are taken from *The Holy Bible*, English Standard Version® (ESV®), copyright © 2001 by Crossway, a publishing ministry of Good News Publishers. Used by permission. All rights reserved. Scripture quotations marked GNT are taken from the Good News Translation in Today's English Version, Second Edition, copyright © 1992 by American Bible Society. Used by permission. Scripture quotations marked MSG are taken from *THE MESSAGE*, copyright © 1993, 1994, 1995, 1996, 2000, 2001, 2002 by Eugene H. Peterson. Used by permission of NavPress. All rights reserved. Represented by Tyndale House Publishers, Inc. Scripture texts in this work marked NAB are taken from the *New American Bible with Revised New Testament and Revised Psalms*, copyright © 1991, 1986, 1970 Confraternity of Christian Doctrine, Washington, D.C., and are used by permission of the copyright owner. All rights reserved. No part of the *New American Bible* may be reproduced in any form without permission in writing from the copyright owner. Scripture quotations marked NASB are taken from the New American Standard Bible,® copyright © 1960, 1962, 1963, 1968, 1971, 1972, 1973, 1975, 1977, 1995 by The Lockman Foundation. Used by permission. Scripture quotations marked NKJV are taken from the New King James Version,® copyright © 1982 by Thomas Nelson, Inc. Used by permission. All rights reserved. Scripture quotations marked NLT are taken from the *Holy Bible*, New Living Translation, copyright © 1996, 2004, 2015 by Tyndale House Foundation. Used by permission of Tyndale House Publishers, Inc., Carol Stream, Illinois 60188. All rights reserved. Scripture quotations marked RSV are taken from the Revised Standard Version of the Bible, copyright © 1952 [2nd edition, 1971] by the Division of Christian Education of the National Council of the Churches of Christ in the United States of America. Used by permission. All rights reserved. Scripture quotations marked KJV are taken from the *Holy Bible*, King James Version. Scripture quotations marked WEB are taken from the World English Bible.

Some of the anecdotal illustrations in this book are true to life and are included with the permission of the persons involved. All other illustrations are composites of real situations, and any resemblance to people living or dead is purely coincidental.

For information about special discounts for bulk purchases, please contact Tyndale House Publishers at csresponse@tyndale.com or call 800-323-9400.

Cataloging-in-Publication Data is available.

ISBN 978-1-61291-582-1

Printed in the United States of America

| 23 | 22 | 21 | 20 | 19 | 18 | 17 |
|----|----|----|----|----|----|----|
| 7 | 6 | 5 | 4 | 3 | 2 | 1 |

*To my brothers, John and Phil*

# CONTENTS

Acknowledgments  *ix*
Introduction  *xi*

1. Ma's Wedding Ring, Dad's Hellevision  *1*
2. The Yellow-Painted Pot-Metal Boudoir Light  *17*
3. Rocks  *25*
4. The Dreaded Four-Way  *39*
5. The Family Bible at Family Prayer  *51*
6. Upright Piano and Soundtrack for the Soul  *71*
7. Polio Braces  *79*
8. Yellow Cheese  *87*
9. Sweet's Liniment  *95*
10. Lye Soap  *103*
11. Mounds, Mars Bars, and the County Home  *109*
12. The Mystery Bag and the Curiosity Cabinet  *119*
13. Extra Plate at the Table  *127*
14. Dad's Rolltop Desk and His Secret Compartment  *135*
15. Gramma's Green Porcelain Wood Stove  *147*
16. The Doctor's Script  *155*
17. Nautical Door  *163*
18. Grandfather's Chair  *171*
19. Glover's Mange Cure  *175*

20. Potlucks  *183*
21. Chocolate Éclairs  *187*
22. The Wringer  *191*
23. Matchboxes and Sawdust  *203*
24. Lumps in the Mattress  *211*

Conclusion: The Kite  *221*
Notes  *224*

# ACKNOWLEDGMENTS

Iam often called a "trend-spotter." I hate that. I see myself as someone who rummages around in the attic of Christianity as part of a rescue operation for the obscure and forgotten. There is nothing so exciting as the discovery of artefacts and practices, rituals and images that we forgot we had. I am unimpressed by reputation, but I am impressed by the potential of the "left behind" to point to Jesus' healing power in people's lives, to reveal stories and images that tell us more about God's world and Jesus' saving grace, and to animate Jesus' presence in our lives and the world. Metaphors do that for us. In other words, I run a homeless shelter and orphanage for lost stories and abandoned images. In this book I take you on a personal tour of the mementos that formed my faith, especially as a "PK" where the "preacher" was my mother.

My greatest wealth is my childhood. I am the oldest of three boys, born as close in age as possible for what today would be called "geriatric pregnancies." As you can imagine, the Sweet household was not always high in GDP (Gross Domestic Peace) with Leonard Ira, Philip Dale, and John David running about.

Though I was the eldest, my parents never let any of the

three of us feel that I was the "firstborn" while they were the "after-borns." In many ways, just the opposite was true, as Mother's avowed favorite ("for theological reasons") was the "youngest." We were the "three musketeers"—united in brotherhood. Yet there were many times when my brothers and I resembled less "brotherly love" than "desperados."

Sometimes we were desperados against notoriously strict parents. Sometimes we formed ad hoc desperado alliances against a brother or a cousin. Far from a "mum-with-oldest-son" thing, I was a lone desperado as a teenager, rebelling the most openly and vocally against parental tyranny, which made everyone shake their heads in disbelief when I took Mother into my home and cared for her in the last eleven years of her life. In short, conflict is as much a part of family relationships, including the Sweet family's, as harmony is. It's a fine line that separates blood brothers from bloody desperados.

Like so much of every childhood, mine is half remembered, half imagined. I have sent copies of the chapters that follow to my desperado brothers, Phil and John. This is in part to resist what Mark Twain said about *The Adventures of Tom Sawyer*: "Mostly a true book, with some stretchers." It is amazing how three brothers can grow up in the same household, have the same experiences together, and live in different worlds. Some of what Phil and John remember never even made it into my consciousness. Phil thinks some of what I remember was only a dream he had once. John, who comes the closest to having total recall, has no memory whatsoever of some of it. We were shaped by common events, but those "common events" sometimes had exactly opposite impacts on each of us. As an expression of my gratitude for their help in writing this book, I dedicate it to my two brothers.

Writing this book was a true "soul tsunami." When the seismic shocks on my soul almost became too much to bear, Teri Hyrkas seemed always to sense I needed her shots of *spizzerinctum* to keep me on my quest. Lori Wagner read every word here multiple times and always found new ways for me to open Mother's memory box and to mix and mingle my own story with her journals, artefacts, and biblical notations.

Elizabeth forced me to come to terms with certain features of my growing up as only a wife could. For example, Mother believed that boys should be able to have dolls just as girls do. So each of us had toy guns (which we could never point at a person), but we also had a "companion"—something I had suppressed. When we were very little, my brothers and I would dress and undress in Mother's clothes and use the staircase as our catwalk without any accusation of silliness (a word that used to mean "holy," by the way) by parents who enjoyed the "worldly show." I mention it here so I don't have to mention it in the book itself, hoping most people don't read the acknowledgments.

My editor David Zimmerman, who is one of the humblest people you'll ever meet, is someone Mother would have adopted as her fourth boy. David doesn't know how good he is, which Mother would have loved. She believed that self-praise is another word for boasting is another word for body odor. In a world where BO is the new cologne, Mother believed that self-deprecating humor was the best deodorant. She would have loved the smell of David Zimmerman.

This book fits no known genre or category, something that runs like an *obligato* across the story of Mother's life. If NavPress publisher Don Pape had not believed in this book and my agent Mark Sweeney hadn't been convinced that hybridity could be holy, this book would not be in your hands right now.

Every generation has a "good ol' times" delusion. For Mother the "good ol' times" were in the future. I am proud to be my mother's son, and I have written this book so that our kids and their kids, even though they may not have known Mabel Velma Boggs Sweet, will be proud to be her descendants—Leonard Jr., Justin, Thane, Soren, Egil, Joshua, Zachary, Sarah, Matthias, Nikolas, Caden, Conor, Lucas, Ellie, James, Angelina, Asher, and Gabriel. That's fourteen boys and four of the strongest women you'll ever meet. Mother's heritage continues.

*Leonard Sweet*
*Thanksgiving Day, 2016*

# INTRODUCTION

*From now on, think of it this way: Sin speaks a dead
language that means nothing to you; God speaks your
mother tongue, and you hang on every word. You are
dead to sin and alive to God. That's what Jesus did.*

ROMANS 6:11, MSG

Mothers cast long, long shadows.

Mark Twain famously told would-be authors to
"write what you know." I have never taken that advice, pre-
ferring to write about what I don't know so that in the process of writing I can reduce my ignorance. But in this book
I am living out Twain's dictum. I am writing what I know:
my mother, Mabel Boggs Sweet (20 March 1912–26 July
1993).[1]

To my everlasting shame, I never fully appreciated Mother
when she was alive. But this book is more than an offering
on the altar of mea culpa. It is my attempt to give Mother—
fiery holiness preacher, passionate follower of Jesus, and
driven woman before her time—a voice. It's an exercise in
literary ventriloquism, a jointly authored act of collaboration

between the living and the dead. In these pages, I consort with my mother's words and add a quantity of my own—the only time I could get, you might say, a word in edgewise. As such, it is part memoir, part dialogue with ancestors and descendants, part theological reverie, part devotional, and part window into the material culture of the world of an evangelical empire that died in my lifetime. It is based on the belief that we each will be judged, not by where we end up but by how far we have come from where we started—while staying in, not straying from or entirely repudiating, our origins.

I am telling Mother's story by means of what I call the keyhole method of theology: Peer through a narrow aperture to see the whole; find in the particular the best path to the universal. The small hole in the fence is what best opens up the big picture, big concepts, big mysteries, big possibilities, big stories, big insights, big truths, big introductions to other worlds. I learned this methodology from the Arcades Project of the German philosopher and Jewish cultural critic Walter Benjamin (1892–1940), who exhorted the historian to "discover in the analysis of the small individual moment the crystal of the total event."[2] A whole life can be examined synecdochically through a bowl or a chair or a book or a key. I have also learned this from the comedies of Jerry Seinfeld and the novels and essays of Nicholson Baker, both of which showcase how the mundane details and minute things of life prove a remarkably rich source of pleasure and comedy and insight.

I have chosen twenty-four keyholes to ponder. Each keyhole is an arcane artefact. Let me explain what I mean by those three words: *ponder, arcane,* and *artefact.*

First, *arcane. Arcane* comes from the Latin *arca,* signifying a chest in which something special is locked away. Our "arcanum" is a treasure box where life's most precious secrets are kept and where ordinary things are infused with metaphysical significance by something called "pondering." In the "arcane" cubbyholes of life, some things become "transparent things" (to use the title of Nabokov's late novella);[3] something like a touch or a smell of a thing comes to carry time itself. Kenneth Clark suggests that there are two kinds of collectors: "those who aim at completing a series, and those who long to possess things that have bewitched them."[4] He missed a third: those who bring something back, who open up the arcane to mark a memory and store a story. We all are that third kind of "collector": acquisitive connoisseurs of stories. The best gifts are our "arcana," our used items, heirlooms haloed with memories, stuff "stuffed" with stories.

Second, *ponder.* The word *sunballousa* is Greek for "placing together for comparison," which we translate as "ponder."[5] Luke's Gospel says that Mary "treasured all these things in her heart."[6] What things? The angel Gabriel's words. Cousin Elizabeth's words. The shepherds' words. The Scriptures' words about the Messiah's coming. Every evolving event, every new word, might yield more light to this astonishing unfolding. So Mary kept adding to her "arcanum," to her treasure store. She bundled all that was happening into a precious box. "Pondering" meant she unpacked the contents of that box over and over again and spread the items out on the table of her heart. Each time, she would arrange the pieces anew, placing the various elements in fresh configurations. One day she would, perhaps, place the shepherds' words beside a passage from a Hebrew prophet. The next day, she might place the shepherds' words beside the words of Gabriel. On the Sabbath day she might consider the shepherds' words as they related to Elizabeth's greeting. Mary reverently held each word to the light and compared it with the other treasures in her bag.[7]

---

*God is not in the business of preserving Calvinism, Methodism, or any other "ism." God only must preserve Calvary.*

MABEL BOGGS SWEET

---

Third, *artefact*. Protestantism effected an estrangement between people and things, faith and artefacts. Lutheranism was not as energized about the role of imagery and iconography as Calvinism,[8] a wing of the Reformation obsessed about false worship and anxious to drive people into the Word and away from distractions like the arts. Iconographic vandalism was part of early Calvinism's identity, and the dramatic outrageousness of much Baroque religious art is a reaction against Protestant iconoclasm. Evangelicalism is still awash in Puritan whitewash, as exemplified in mega-church warehouses, barren of religious imagery, dotting the landscapes of suburbia.

To be sure, Christianity finds expression not only in intellectual forms (doctrines), visual forms (art), and ritual forms (liturgy) but also in material, tangible forms, while transcending all of these.[9] There is no faith and no church but in things—at least no Christian faith or church. The greatest "object" in history is the body of Christ himself. We are taught to feel at one with a person, with a body, and to unite ourselves to a "thing," an object, that is brought to life by another "thing," the breath of the Spirit. Samuel Johnson, in the preface to his 1755 *Dictionary*, reminded his readers what he had learned after nine years of research into what some have called the greatest work of scholarship in Western history. "Words," he writes, quoting an anonymous contemporary, "are the daughters of earth, and . . . things are the sons of heaven."

Paul said that compared to "the supreme good of knowing Christ Jesus," everything else in life was but "rubbish," or *skubalon* (really "sewage").[10] Yet we know that no one had a more incarnational sense of the presence of Christ or the sacramental nature of creation than Paul. All being is blessed. Nothing corporeal or material is alien to the divine. Our material environment is special to God. The false dichotomy between the material and the spiritual prevents us from seeing how the material is spiritual and the spiritual is material.

At the end of his second letter to Timothy, Paul asks for some *things*—some clothing and books (parchments, scrolls)—that he had left behind.[11] So "things" aren't useless or "sewage" in themselves; they are valuable insofar as they add to the story of knowing Jesus and "the power of his resurrection."[12] Walt Whitman wrote,

> *There was a child went forth every day,*
> *And the first object he look'd upon, that object he*
> *     became.*[13]

That's why we feast our eyes first upon Christ.

The three-tiered wedding cake with white royal icing, yellow marzipan, and Georgian pillars is supposed to be a "traditional wedding cake." But the "tradition" only became standard in the 1890s. The ceremonial slicing by bride and groom is unknown before the early twentieth century, and doubtless it derives from the fact that to support upper layers the icing must be hard as rock. Cutting it required a saw or brute force, so late-Victorian confectioners created a scene that was later rationalized with ubiquitous photography capturing the first cut, which came to symbolize conjugal collaboration or even virginal union. Notice what comes first: The human imagination creates objects and other "things that matter."[14] Then comes a metaphorical handle for the object, which puts it to use. What comes next is the story or meaning of that object, as expressed in words and gestures—the last stop on the creativity highway.

Everything material, every "material thing," has a message. You just need a listening heart or semiotic stethoscope to hear the story. Things are worth keeping around and prizing when they add to the story. If they don't add to the story, they are hindrances and nothing but "stuff." Houses filled with "pretty, pointless, expensive things," as Amy Bloom puts it in her novel *Lucky Us*,[15] breed people who are storyless and soulless and lead pointless lives.

People need to finger relics, leavings, fixtures, fittings. The Amish have a saying that "what you take into your hand you take into your heart." Sherry Turkle challenges us to "consider objects as companions to our emotional lives or as provocations to thought. . . . We think with the objects we love; we love the objects we think with."[16] Objects are the bridges that connect emotion and reason, the right brain and the left brain. You might even call objects our corpus callosum. Thinking with objects is the epitome of concrete thinking, the opposite of abstract thinking.

As a pianist, I fell in love with the keys. I loved the feel of the ivory and the pedal as much as I loved to think musically and compose, with the black and white keys, new stories of the wideness of God's mercy and the wonder of God's world. In the final years of his life, the long-deaf Beethoven based his musical judgments on his piano students' playing by watching their hands moving on the keys and their feet pumping the pedals. Beethoven connected the sights of fingers and muscles moving on an object to his musical memories of that same object.

Objects matter not just because we see them but often because we don't. The anthropologist Daniel Miller proposes that material objects are, by their very nature, recessive. Things have a way of disappearing into the background, where they provide a stage set for social interactions, silently shaping the terms of human engagement.[17] Scholars are now even talking about "thing theory," as certain objects get invested with meaning beyond their material existence.

There is an old story of a tourist's visit to a famous nineteenth-century preacher in England. When the fan arrived at the preacher's home and asked to see the place where the preacher wrote his masterpieces, he was astounded to discover that the "study" consisted only of one simple room, with no furniture except for a single chair. "But where is your furniture?" the tourist asked.

The preacher replied, "Where is yours?"

"Where is mine?" said the puzzled visitor. "I'm only a visitor here—just passing through."

"So am I," answered the preacher. "So am I."

What's wrong with this story, often called on by preachers, is that it simply isn't true. Jesus is "the Savior of the body."[18] Jesus came to save and heal *all* of us—body, mind, spirit. The Christian mission is not the salvation of souls but the salvation of the world.

"To have the right feelings in our souls," Czech scientist and philosopher Václav Cílek has written, "we need physical contact with objects and places."[19] Claude Levi-Strauss, French anthropologist and architect of structuralism, taught us in his exploration of "bricolage" that objects are "goods-to-think-with," which puns in French with "good to think with."[20] Each one of us creates a bricolage of storied objects. Everything you touch, every material thing, is saturated with symbolic meaning and semiotic significance.[21] The meaning of things is not found in the things themselves, but in the stories of the things.

~

There can be love at first sight between two people. Sometimes there is love at first sight between a person and a place. *Topophilia* is the name for the ability to experience the emotional charge of a place—an endangered sensation in a franchised world of homogenization. Nonplaces (such as suburbs) are locations stripped of context and excite no emotional attachment.

But sometimes there is love at first sight between a person and an object. The tactile approach to the material transports us in time, traces the remembrances of things touched, and extracts the tracks of memory. The very fact that after 9/11 the bottom fell out of the antiques market even as the craft industry boomed evidences the fact that making things matters; the patience of a practiced craft treats us psychologically, trains us aesthetically, and matures us theologically.

Do we really think that if teens were making things they would be destroying things so easily? Do we really think we can truly capture memory in digital form? Technologies of memory are being introduced every day that help you embalm the photo of your old baseball glove. But the smell of that old baseball glove triggers memories that photos and digits can't match.

Material for memory should be material in some fashion. The Christian faith is the practice of bricolage. A Christian is a bricoleur, a practitioner of the concrete, a ponderer of the arcane, an artist of artefacts such as a table or tumbler, out of which, in the words of Sylvia Plath, "a certain minor light may still / Leap incandescent."[22]

Italian sociologist Antonio Gramsci (1891–1937), who has taught me so much about history but so little about life, claimed we are products of a historical process that has "deposited in [us] an infinity of traces, without leaving an inventory."[23] You might call this book you're now holding one attempt at retrieving that inventory, but it's more than that. I did not choose the objects in this inventory because they are relics from my past or talismans for my dreams.[24] Rather, this book is an exercise in what the Greeks called *ekphrasis*, which means to "speak out" (as contrasted with *synphrasis*, which means to "speak with"). Medieval writers loved *ekphrasis* and earmarked art, relics, and eucharistic items as worthy of speaking for themselves and speaking into our lives. In *ekphrasis* the focus is less on the object than on the viewer, whose trajectory is changed by contemplation of the object.[25]

The Amish, and the Shakers before them, taught that whether carving, caning, or canning, human creativity draws forth the divine and radiates back the Creator's love for us. If things can be transmitters of transcendence, the chapters that follow share twenty-four "things" that have given my life a sustaining narrative and taken hold of my heart. A thing-filled heart is not necessarily a hollow heart if those "things" are storied icons like the ones to which you are about to be introduced.

The life of faith is not one of uninterrupted splendor but of the resplendence of the common, the glory of the ordinary, the marvel of a table hosting people eating, a country road taking in bikers, a field receiving hikers, a seashore impressed by footsteps, a bed engulfing lovers, a ball being tossed successfully by your favorite team, a helping hand extended to another, or a runway to an altar and the Eucharist. This is what is truly called "theology."

The chapters that follow lift out artefacts from my memory box that tell the story of an early woman preacher, a church planter, and a lay theologian: my mother. If you had to tell the story of your life or your family, which items would you pick? I chose a wedding ring, a TV, rocks, leather straps, a Bible, a piano, liniment, braces, soap, a candy bar, a dinner plate, a desk, cheese, a cast-iron stove, shampoo, a nautical door, a chair, an eclair, a washing machine, a matchbox, sawdust, a mattress, and a lamp. These are my stories—my mother's life, handed down to me in heirlooms. Thank you for joining me in opening my memory box.

# 1

# MA'S WEDDING RING, DAD'S HELLEVISION

*O Lord, let me not yearn for power seats or judgment*
*seats but for the towel of washing feet.*

MABEL BOGGS SWEET

There is an old German proverb:

*Pastor's children and miller's cows*
*turn out badly, furrow brows.*

I have furrowed many a brow during my career as a preacher's kid.

The preacher in my household was my mother, Mabel Velma Boggs. She was a formidable mother and an ordained minister in the Pilgrim Holiness Church. My brother Phil likes to tell people we grew up on Paris Island, where recruits get basic training in the Marines. The Pilgrim Holiness

Church was the Marine Corps of Methodism. They just wanted a few totally committed people, and our home was one of their boot camps.

Brought up a strict Methodist in the hills of southeastern West Virginia, at age seventeen Mabel Boggs was converted in a parking lot after attending a revival meeting led by a visiting Pilgrim Holiness evangelist. The second-oldest of seven surviving children (five died in childhood), her father ("G. L.") insisted that she continue her piano playing and her leadership in the Epworth League and attend the Methodist church with the rest of the family. She responded by defying her father, who called her a "killjoy" and a "spoilsport" (among other things). But after a year of Mabel's stubborn witnessing, the entire Boggs household moved en masse to join a new Pilgrim Holiness church plant in Covington, Virginia, a town right across the state line from the place in West Virginia where the family homestead was located.

As an "eleventh-hour laborer," Mabel Boggs didn't bother to graduate from high school before enrolling at God's Bible School and Missionary Training Home in Cincinnati. The school had been established in 1900 by the founder of the Pilgrim Holiness Church, Martin Wells Knapp (1853–1901), a Methodist minister who was unhappy with Methodism's increasing "formalism" and decreasing emphasis on what he called "Pentecostal doctrines" like holiness, healing, "special revelation," and the "gathering together unto Him" of "the Coming of the Lord."

This is the same school William Seymour attended for a

year. A Roman Catholic from Louisiana, Seymour grew up believing that visions and dreams were forms of divine communication. These "special revelations" inspired Seymour to seek out Knapp's school, attend his racially and economically inclusive "Revivalist Chapel" in downtown Cincinnati, and take classes for a year at his school before proceeding to San Francisco. There he started the famed Azusa Street Revival that would inaugurate the Third Wave of global Christianity known today as Pentecostalism, which differed from Knapp's understanding of "Pentecostal" only by the inclusion of tongues.

God's Bible School taught one thing: the Bible. Its official motto, and the banner over its ads, was "Back to the Bible." All of its courses revolved around Bible study and how to implement biblical teaching in practical, everyday life. It offered a diploma, not a degree, for those who successfully completed its course of study, and it provided a home base for those preparing to be missionaries. At GBS Mabel Boggs came under the spell of a faculty member who left after a year to teach at another Pilgrim Holiness school. She followed her mentor to Allentown Bible School in Pennsylvania (later called United Wesleyan College) and began theological training in earnest. But the more she studied, the more she doubted her faith and even her salvation. After a two-year dark-night/dry-well spell, she came to a point where, in her words, she had to either "lay it all on the altar" or leave school.

There were four things Mabel confessed to having to "lay down," with each of them progressively more difficult. First, was she willing to lay down her reputation—her need to be liked and approved by others? Would she serve, not those who wanted her the most, but those who needed her the most?

Second, was she willing to lay down her marital status? Was she willing to be single, to die an "old maid"?

Third, was she willing to lay down her ambition to be used by God? Was she open to *not* being used by God, but simply to live and die a faithful disciple?

The fourth was the hardest, she later testified: Was she willing to put the church on the altar, to lay down her beloved Pilgrim Holiness church, and simply follow Jesus?

When she said yes to all four, when she "laid it all on the altar," Mabel Velma Boggs had an experience of entire sanctification and began living the "way of holiness" and full salvation. The very act of laying down everything she held dear gave her the power to pick up a life of doing the very things she had "laid down": church planting, home mission work, musical evangelism, the dream of foreign missions work, and marriage.

Shortly after graduating from Allentown Bible School, Mabel Boggs started her tent-making ministry. She went to work in the Newport News Shipbuilding and Drydock Company, boarding with a family at 225 Chesapeake Avenue while she planted a Pilgrim Holiness (now Wesleyan) church.[1] Her church-planting partner was Walden C. Hall, who today lives in Roanoke, Virginia. He alternated weeks for preaching with Mother, but they sang together in a mixed quartet that toured throughout Virginia and West Virginia. When I finally tracked down Walden in 2014 and heard his reminiscences, one of his first comments was, "I can remember vividly the day and hour I met your mother." Mother was nothing if not memorable.

---

*The high priests tried to hush the resurrection. They tried to hush the disciples: "Speak no further" (Acts 4:17). They took steps to eliminate the disciples as they did Jesus (Acts 5:33). They lost in Jesus' case. They lost in the disciples' case (Acts 5:39). They lose in our case also.*

MABEL BOGGS SWEET

---

It was in the course of planting this church in Warwick, Virginia, that my mother met my father, Leonard Lucius Sweet. He was a radar operator stationed at Langley Air Force Base in Newport News, Virginia. Both were in their midthirties, my mother two years older than my father. Neither had ever been married.

In 1945 Rev. Boggs was speaking on "Five Words from the Lord" at a revival meeting in Newport News. Her challenge was simple: Why do we reduce faith to a bare minimum rather than expand faith to maximum range and uttermost spirit? That evening the Spirit descended on those assembled in a special way, and a backsliding, moviegoing soldier from upstate New York, who for some reason had gone to the revival that evening, found his heart "strangely warmed"—by both the Spirit and the preacher.

At first my Free Methodist father got nowhere with his overtures for courtship. My Pilgrim Holiness preacher mother from the mountain hollers of West Virginia (where "Yankee" was never just one word) insisted that the Bible clearly said, "Be ye not unequally yoked together with unbelievers."[2] For her, my father's Adirondack Mountain roots were enough "unbelief" to disqualify him from any serious consideration. Second, if she was in the Marines (Pilgrim Holiness), then he was in the Army.

But Leonard Sweet was as persistent as Mabel Boggs was principled. He continued to pursue her as she waited to be "released" from her itinerant ministry by a biblical directive.[3] As she told the story, one day she was debating what to do about her gentleman caller, and as she read her Bible according to the "lucky dip" method (what the ancient church called "sortilege"), her finger landed on Deuteronomy 2:3: "You have been traversing these mountains long enough. Turn towards the North" (Mother's translation, or MT).

Some people have a "life verse." My brothers and I have a literal life verse. We are alive today because of a verse of Scripture.

In a letter dated 12 October 1945 to "Sargent [*sic*] Leonard L. Sweet"—who was receiving letters at 133 North Arlington Avenue, Gloversville, New York—Mother accepted Dad's proposal. But not until she had made it clear that this would be a missional marriage; it would "submit" to God first and foremost. It was a relationship in the spirit of William Wilberforce, who had so integrated his faith into his everyday life that during his honeymoon he took his bride on a tour of Hannah More's Sunday schools.[4]

Despite being "released," Mabel Boggs Sweet never really left the ministry. Even after she was married, she wrote in her journals, "Let your goal be Christ not a husband." She made it clear in her journals that it was never simply that God led her into this marriage with Leonard. It was always "God brought me to Gloversville" or God "brought me to this place." She needed to "find her place" in this new place of mission.

~

Throughout her life, when people asked Mother, "What are your interests?", she would frequently reply, "The will of God and people are my interests." She kept her ordination and accepted speaking engagements at revivals whenever she could. But her new ministry became the raising of three boys in the "ways of holiness."

For Mother, the family was a domestic church, and she was the pastor. She let us know that as much as she loved "her boys" (as she called us), she had "laid it all on the altar," including us, and put Jesus first. We came second. (Where Dad fit in I could never figure out, but he didn't seem to mind. He'd take whatever of Mother he could get.) When Mother made an evangelistic witness to someone or visited them in their home, she would report back in her journal the results: either "room for Jesus" or "no room for Jesus."

Mother used to tell us that before any of us were born, when she was serving as an evangelist, God "told" her that she did not have the education to cope with the changes that lay ahead in ministry and the church. But if she would trust God to take her down a different direction—marriage, kids, cleaning, and cooking—God would bless her through her children and use them in ways that she couldn't be used. Mother imbued in her three boys a missionary's sense of destiny, so each of us, as different as we are, all came by a missional mentality naturally.

So Mother's family became her parish, and while she sent us to the public school, she simultaneously homeschooled us in the Christian faith, sending us out the door with these words ringing in our ears: "Children need to be insulated, not isolated." Children should be so prepared and protected by the armor of truth, she believed, that they can actually grow stronger from resisting the enemy.

Coming out of the holiness tradition, sometimes we were called "holy rollers." But Mother taught us to say back to people who mocked us, "I'd rather roll into heaven than dance into hell."

---

*For I am with thee, and no man shall set on thee*
*to hurt thee: for I have much people in this city.*
ACTS 18:10 (KJV)
the verse Mother said God gave her when the
"good church people" of the Pilgrim Holiness Church
and the Free Methodist Church defrocked her

---

In the Pilgrim Holiness church, instead of giving a ring to your fiancée, you gave a watch. "She got her watch" was how you referred to an engaged woman. When a girl showed up in church with a watch, everyone started talking. I once pointed out to Mother, "But the watch is more gold and a bigger circle." Mother smiled as she replied, as if her next words settled everything, "But it's six inches higher, and not around the finger."

The problem with the holiness tribe, Mother felt, was that they spent too much time on minor issues like dress and hair and too little time on major issues like Jesus and holiness. She compared them to physicians who spent all their time diagnosing patients and none of their time on prescribing medicine for the cure. Or as she put it pointedly, "There is more concern about the dress of the bride than the cry of the Bridegroom."[5]

When Mother accepted a ring at her wedding to a "liberal" Free Methodist, and when she bobbed her hair for the ceremony, it was too much for the denominational establishment. Word of what happened reached headquarters, and Mabel Boggs Sweet was brought up by her peers on three charges of worldliness: She had accepted a wedding ring, she had cut and curled her hair, and she had worn lipstick and rouge.[6]

Mother pleaded guilty to the first two offenses but not guilty to the third. The wedding pictures were claimed as "proof positive" that all three charges were true. But Mother pointed out that photographers of the day routinely colored pictures to accent certain features, such as cheeks and lips. In fact, other wedding pictures showed no evidence of cosmetics on her face. The prosecution argued that no photographer would have highlighted those features if they hadn't been highlighted in the first place.

When I heard this story over and over again growing up, I formulated one of the basic facts of life: You can't fix stupid. The just-plain-ignorant will hear "Marvel not" in John's Gospel as "Marble not," and before you know it, it's a sin to play a game of marbles. And no amount of reasoning will change minds.

In spite of a spirited defense by Mother's local church pastor (who later became the head of the denomination), she was found guilty of all charges, defrocked, and subjected to a form of shunning.

My father, who never trusted "those PH people," was not unhappy that we would now migrate over to where his family worshiped: the Free Methodist Church. But my mother thought the Free Methodist weak at the knees, as opposed to the powerful praying of the Pilgrim Holiness people. So even after she had her orders recalled and we were kicked out of the church, she still dragged us to the Pilgrim Holiness prayer meeting on Wednesday nights.

My father refused to go. So it was on Mother to sneak us into the church. We would sit in the last row. Not only did no one speak to us, but one time the ushers were so mad that the Sweet family was still coming to church that they took Mother by the elbow and dragged her out of the church. They picked us boys up, carted us out, and dumped us on the sidewalk with a stern warning to never return. The next Wednesday night, the Sweet family showed up again, but the pastor was present this time, and no usher laid a hand on us.

My impression of ushers growing up in church: a group of men who always and everywhere wore dark suits, black shoes, and serious faces as they passed the plates and grabbed them authoritatively when they reached the end of the aisles. Surely these men, I thought, owned the church.

We kept up this pattern of being a part of two churches: the Free Methodist one, where we attended church on Sunday morning and Sunday evening, youth group and "sword drills" during the week, and Pine Grove Camp meeting every summer; and the Pilgrim Holiness one, where we went to Wednesday-night prayer meetings and Victory Grove Camp meeting every summer, as well as some other holiness camp meetings during the summer, when my father's vacation could accommodate them. Mabel Boggs Sweet received preaching credentials in the Free Methodist Church and spent whatever time she could conducting evangelistic meetings and revivals in the mountains of North Carolina, Virginia, and West Virginia.

This lasted until I was age nine, when Dad succumbed to the blandishments of the devil's blinking box. Up until then we grew up watching the radio. But my father wanted to watch a TV show called *Bonanza*, and my brothers and I wanted to watch a show that aired just before it called

*The Wonderful World of Disney*. It was these two shows that killed Sunday-night worship. All the church had to do was reschedule its Sunday-night services for an hour earlier, but it believed that it could take on pop culture and win. It is a lesson the church is still learning the hard way.

I will never forget the Friday night when Rev. Rudd came calling to see if it was true about the Sweet home invasion by "hellevision." As soon as he crossed the threshold, our pastor dispatched my brothers and me upstairs and told us not to come down until we were instructed otherwise. Being of a recalcitrant nature, I snuck down to the first landing in the staircase and heard everything. With the devil staring him in the face, Rev. Rudd gave my parents an ultimatum: the church or the TV. He would give them until Sunday to decide, if they couldn't decide at that moment. But there was no other alternative in choosing whom we would serve: God or the devil.

I couldn't understand why our pastor was so upset. We only got to watch three hours a week of our own shows, and two of those hours were reserved for *The Howdy Doody Show* by my two brothers. Sometimes mother would put on *Queen for a Day* when she was doing something else, but that was basically it. How could these shows cause such a fuss? (I suspected the *Queen* shows as the culprit, since mother seemed to pretend she wasn't really watching it.)

That Sunday morning, during the announcements, Rev. Rudd asked for a decision from the Sweet family. The church got quiet, and Dad hung his head, refusing to speak. Never one to pass up an opportunity to deliver a sermon, Mother stood up and launched into some of the best preaching of her life. She explained *adiaphora* ("things indifferent") without using the word and made a case for matter as not being evil in itself (only in what we do with it) without ever using the word *Manichaeanism*. She then used the example of the pews we were sitting in: They were heavy and wooden but not evil unless a strong man picked one up and threw it at people. I thought she was getting a little too into this illustration, so I was glad when she sat down.

A short meeting of those ushers followed after church, while we waited outside. The ruling came down: We had been removed from the membership rolls of the Free Methodist Church. That meant Mother's preaching credentials would be declared null and void as well. If I heard "you can't fix stupid" from the Pilgrims, I heard from the Frees that "there is always someone who hears truth as treason."

This is how I became a United Methodist. They'll take anyone. And they warmly took the Sweet family. After getting kicked out of "the best churches in town," I grew to appreciate the graciousness and spaciousness of the United Methodist church. To quote the psalmist, "O Lord, thou has set my foot in a spacious room."[7]

The shunning that took place after we were kicked out of the Free Methodist Church was in some ways harsher than the shunning by the Pilgrim Holiness people. Some of my father's relatives (including his sister and stepmother) were in this church, and for many years we could not enter my aunt's house or play with my cousins. We exchanged presents on the front porch of the house where my Gramma May and Aunt Charlotte lived.

The emotional civil war of always feeling like an alien took its toll on Mother. The first verse God gave her when she was banned and shunned by the Free Methodists was Luke 9:34: "While he was speaking, a cloud appeared and covered them, and they were afraid as they entered the cloud."

No matter how great the fear, the cloud was needed for growth. The cloud was needed to face oneself. The cloud was needed to give voice and place to Jesus. The cloud was needed to prepare for the needy in the valley. The cloud was needed to make truth clear and uncontaminated by our own opinions. The cloud was needed to save us from bitterness. In Mother's words, "It's what you learn in the cloud that will bless in the valley."

When the loneliness and depression became almost unbearable, when the church in Gloversville was so against her, God gave Mother a second verse, a verse so tender to her she could hardly talk about it or recite it: "For I am with you, and no one is going to attack and harm you, because I have many people in this city."[8] It would not be those in the church who would save her. It would be those in the city, in the world, whom God would use to protect and preserve her.

Sometimes God is more active in the world than in the church. A powerful expression of this is Vincent Van Gogh's *Starry Night*. If you look at the sky in that painting, you can tell these are turbulent times. In the midst of all the confusion and fear, the houses in the painting are "lit up." But the lights in the church are out.

To this day, I fail miserably at living up to ideological blueprints, political correctitudes, or theological cutouts for a reason.

Because the Methodist church had no Sunday-night service or Wednesday-night prayer meeting, Mother insisted that we still go to Sunday-night service at the Free Methodist Church. Once again, no one—except kids our age who didn't know better—would speak to us. So, by the time I had reached nine years of age, we went to the Methodist Church on Sunday morning, the Free Methodist church on Sunday nights, and the Pilgrim Holiness church on Wednesday nights for prayer meeting. To a kid it didn't seem that we were getting kicked out of churches so much as we were picking up churches.

The best thing for my brothers and me was that now we had three summer camps to attend: Skye Farm Methodist Camp in Warrensburg, New York; Pine Grove Free Methodist Camp in Saratoga Springs, New York; and Victory Grove Camp outside of Albany, New York.

~

In 2015, both the Free Methodists and the Pilgrim Holiness churches (now Wesleyan Church) celebrated Mother, formally apologizing for their treatment of her and, in the case of the Free Methodists, restoring her ministerial credentials.

Even though her restoration came twenty-plus years after her death, it was a proud moment for me as her son to receive the church's *nostra culpa* on her behalf. I wish it had been more like the vindication of Mary Mackillop (1842–1909), also known as St. Mary of the Cross, Australia's singular canonized saint. She is the only person in the history of Christianity who has gone from excommunication to canonization in her lifetime. She was excommunicated partly because she was not acting as the Roman Catholic Church thought a woman should act. Mother never did either.

In 2004 I was asked to address the General Conference of the Wesleyan Church in Indianapolis. I would have moved heaven and earth to accept this invitation (and I did), because at the time I saw it as the ultimate vindication of Mother. But just before I went to the assembly hall to deliver my keynote address, I stopped by the bookstore, which featured a new volume directly from the Wesleyan Publishing House: *Celebrate Our Daughters: 150 Years of Women in Wesleyan Ministry.*[9] I bought it in a hurry, and on my way to the stage, I checked to see whether there was an entry for Mabel Boggs Sweet. There was none by that name, but under "Mabel Boggs" there was, featuring dates, places of ministry, and an invitation: "If you know anything more about this woman preacher, please be in touch with us."

When I stood up to preach that evening, I had my Bible in one hand and that book in the other. Guess which one I read from first?

# 2
# THE YELLOW-PAINTED
# POT-METAL BOUDOIR LIGHT

<hr>

*A diamond is not beautiful because it's a diamond,*
*but it's beautiful because it stood the pressure.*
MABEL BOGGS SWEET, 12 MARCH 1979

Mother "made do" with the little she had. We had foot-stools fashioned out of tomato cans in our home. Mother took large tomato cans, tied them together with string and twine, wrapped them in discarded cloths, and sewed some recycled fabric around them to make them look like normal footstools. You didn't want to put your head on them, however.

Almost everything in the Sweet household was hand-me-down, make-do, or recycled rubble. Even the piano was a dilapidated upright that couldn't keep in tune for more than a few days. There were two exceptions, two "nice" things in our house. One was my father's rolltop desk, which he had inherited from his father. The other was my mother's small, yellow-painted boudoir light, which she inherited from her mother. Even though the paint was chipping off the pot-metal, and one of the small stained-glass panels was chipped, and an armature was bent, this one little boudoir light was my toehold on beauty amidst an aesthetic of disrepair and dilapidation.

When Mabel Boggs Sweet was no longer in active church ministry but was raising a family, she called herself the "Minister of Small Things." When people asked her, "What are your interests?", she would often reply, "The ministry of small things." Then she would launch into a dissertation on how, as she put it, "God is so abundant in giving, yet God can narrow our service down to small things that accomplish his will." Her go-to Scripture was Zechariah 4:10: "Who dares despise the day of small things?" She would recite it as a dare.

---

*You must prove yourself faithful in little for*
*God to trust you to be faithful in much.*
MABEL BOGGS SWEET

---

Mother took seriously the notion that "the hand that rocks the cradle rules the world." She would tell people that the role of every mother raising children was greater in God's eyes than that of the President of the United States. Mother turned her reading of the Bible into a homiletic litany:

*For God to produce a John the Baptist,*
*    He had to have an Elizabeth*
*For God to have a Samuel,*
*    He had to have a Hannah*
*For God to have a Moses,*
*    He had to have a Jacabed*
*For God to give to the world a Savior,*
*    He had to have a Mary.*
*For God to save England from war and raise up a John Wesley,*
*    He had to have a Susanna Wesley.*

"Where are these people to be formed?" she would ask rhetorically. "Not in seminary. In homes around the table."

From the day we were born, she would say, "My boys belong to Jesus, not to me." Mother made it clear that the business of raising cradle Catholics, or bassinet Baptists, or manger Methodists, or Graco GARBs, or playpen Presbyterians, or whatever the denomination of the day might be, was an inferior mission. Ultimately only Jesus satisfies, only Jesus can saturate and satiate the human heart; and her rocking the cradle was nothing more—or less—than cradling the Rock. Jesus is not about something. Jesus is that something itself.

---

*I am too small for the mission I am called to do, but my God*
*is able to fill my smallness until I can fulfill my mission.*
MABEL BOGGS SWEET

---

The Bible is tied together by stories of people taking what is in their hands, however little or large, and trusting God to make something good of it. That is the biblical understanding of "success." If you can take what you have and make do with it for God and good, that's success. If you can't take what you have and make do with it for good and God, that's failure. You live the gospel in little things, or you don't live it at all.

As if to carve the theology of littleness on our souls, one of the first songs Mother had us sing was a children's song. We all had to memorize the lyrics before we knew most of its stories or even the meaning of the words:

> *Shamgar had an oxgoad, David had a sling,*
> *Dorcas had a needle, Rahab had some string,*
> *Samson had a jawbone, Aaron had a rod,*
> *Mary had some ointment, and they all were*
> *used of God.*[1]

One of Mother's favorite songs (which I never tagged as a children's song because she sang it so much herself) was this one:

> *We are building ev'ry day,*
> *At our work and at our play:*
> *Not with hammer, blow on blow,*
> *Not the timber sawing so;*
> *Building a house not made with hands,*

*Following Father's perfect plans:*
*Little builders all are we,*
*Building for eternity.*[2]

As Mother read her Bible, it told a metanarrative of God doing little large, of the wisest words coming out of the most illiterate mouths from the lowliest places. Those who have nothing share everything. Those who have everything share nothing.

---

*A thing can be small because of its ideas, not because of its*
*numbers. Its numbers may be large, but it still be small. And*
*vice versa. Here is one small baby. Who is this? There is nothing*
*larger than this. This is God's love tied up in a bundle of flesh.*

MABEL BOGGS SWEET

---

Mother honored the Twelve and made us learn the names of all twelve by memorizing as early as we could the following Sunday school ditty:

*There were twelve disciples Jesus called to help Him:*
*Simon Peter, Andrew, James, his brother John;*
*Philip, Thomas, Matthew, James the son of Alphaeus,*
*Simon, Thaddeus, Judas, and Bartholomew.*
*Jesus calls us too, Jesus calls us too;*
*We are His disciples, I am one and you;*

*Jesus calls us too, Jesus calls us too;*
*We are His disciples, We His work must do.*[3]

There were male apostles—the Twelve—but Mother insisted there were also women apostles who worked alongside the men. I don't think Mother ever knew that Mary Magdalene carries the official title "apostle to the Apostles" in the Roman Catholic church, but she did remind us that Mary Magdalene was one of a group of women who traveled with Jesus and ministered to his needs. Joanna and Susanna traveled with the Twelve and provided for them out of their own resources (Luke 8:1-3). These women watched the Crucifixion from afar (Luke 23:49) while the Twelve were hiding; these women returned to anoint Jesus' body (Luke 24:1). The three of them proclaimed the good news of the Resurrection to the apostles, forming for Mother an apostleship of Mary Magdalene, Susanna, and Joanna.

In Jesus' relationships with women (as with children, which is another story), Mother found prime examples of Jesus doing large missions with what the world deemed "little" instruments. If the Lord couldn't find a big man, she liked to say (citing Deborah as her prime example), he used a woman. When I'm told I'm a "model preacher," I still remember what Mother said the word *model* meant: "a small imitation of the real thing."

Some of the earliest children's books we read were "little" books: *Chicken Little* and *The Little Engine That Could*.

Large battles are won and lost on little things, and history hinges on the tiniest of joints.

Taste a little honey during the rout? You lose.

Bury some "spoils" of battle, such as a Babylonian mantle and some gold and silver? You lose.

Hold up the hands of your leader? You win.

Hear a gentle whisper in the tops of poplar trees? You win.

Reach into a pouch and fumble out a white stone? You win.

Craft some models of the rats and tumors afflicting you with plagues and droughts? You win.

Barbecue oxen on the hill of Zion? You win.

Take a sacred box into your home? You win.[4]

Each of these stories points not to some causal relationship but to the ordinary signs of God's providence and protection. It's the little things that make the biggest difference. The smaller the strawberry, the juicier it is. Life is one long strand of "such a little thing."

Jesus can be right in our midst but helpless to heal and speechless to save because of our selfish eyes, closed minds, low faith, and small expectations.

---

*God has no bounds.*
*For religion to restrict God is irreligious.*
MABEL BOGGS SWEET

---

Look at the picture on the cover of a seed packet. Does anyone really expect the flower you're growing or the vegetable you're raising to look like that? How many promises go unrealized or unfulfilled? But what you grow from that tiny seed may actually be more of a miracle than the picture on the packet, since you may have had to contend with drought, or bad soil, or weather conditions that no one expected or could control.

Holiness starts small. Like a seed. But holiness has heft. It is not a definition or a designation but a destination and a disposition.

# 3

# ROCKS

*The issue is not "How big is your world?"*
*but "How big is your heart?"*
MABEL BOGGS SWEET

I am a product of mountain culture. Whether in the Allegheny Mountains on the Boggs side or the Adirondack Mountains on the Sweet side, I grew up addicted to the orgy of oxygen one finds only in the mountains.

But one mountain range was clearly more sacred than any other. Even while my father nestled our home in the foothills of the Adirondacks, we grew up with a curious sense of living in exile. For our mother it was almost as if this was an unwritten prenuptial agreement: Ma would live in the Adirondacks, but as often as possible and every summer, Dad had to get her back to Appalachia.

In this Google world, we have forgotten how to dwell,

to live in our landscape. We stand apart from our context in a state of perpetual homelessness. The destiny of digital culture seems as far as you can get from Martin Heidegger's "being in the world" or "dwelling in the world," making *nostalgia* in its truest meaning of "pain" almost impossible.

The term *nostalgia* was coined by Johannes Hofer in 1688 for a disease from which young Swiss soldiers had died: wasting away while deprived of their homeland. The word combines the Greek *nostos* ("return to the native land") with *algos* (implying suffering or grief). When Mother was not dwelling in her sacred landscape, she waxed nostalgic and pined.

Although some of my best memories of growing up are mountain memories, West Virginia functions in my mind as a place of cultural rootedness more than actual physical roots. And as anyone who has ever followed Mountaineers football or basketball can testify, love for West Virginia is not for the weak of body or soul. Be prepared for passionate disappointment and perpetual heartbreak, even when the teams make it to the finals.

As much as Mother would swoon over her favorite white-barked birch trees, which were prevalent in the Adirondacks but which we never saw in the South, she wasn't "home" unless she was enfolded in the everlasting arms of the mountain-mamas of West Virginia. Life was best lived close to nature's bosom.

God speaks the languages of nature and art. Both languages, while illuminating and inspiring, are limited. Mother was closer to the language of nature than of art. In her mind, when you cease to delight in the luminosity of God's creation, when you cease to feel gratitude for the omnipresence of beauty, you fail to honor and praise God. Mother had no idea of semiotics or the Bulgarian-French philosopher Tzvetan Todorov. But in her mind, everything in the world that God had to do with was by definition "fantastic." This meant that although there might be a rational explanation for a thing or event, beyond the rational was always a supra-rational, fantastical explanation that defied the facts. This, for her, was more compelling than the rational explanation.

For Mother (and maybe for John Wesley as well, who made forty-nine of his poems into hymns), the only person who could write lines for God was George Herbert (1593–1633), the Welsh-born poet and Anglican priest. Herbert called creation "either our cupboard of food / or cabinet of pleasure."[1] Mother's natal story may have been living proof of Herbert's couplet, as her love of rocks and advocacy of a GOOD faith (GOOD as an acronym for "Get Out Of Doors") was birthed by bringing the cabinet and cupboard together. My grandparents, George Lemuel Boggs and Ida Blanch McCarty, liked to go coon-hunting together. (At that time, deer were almost extinct, shot to the point of scarcity by mountaineers who loved their deer meat.) It was on one of these "put-food-on-the-table" hunting expeditions that Mother was born "under a rock," as they liked to kid her.[2]

When there was money (one Christmas we all got just

one orange), we received one toy for Christmas. Usually that toy was given to promote our interest in science: an atomic energy lab, a Gilbert chemistry set, a microscope, a rocket-launcher erector set. Our home's hospitality to the role of science in unpacking nature, which helped us better understand God, has made me weary of people pitting religion and science against each other. There is more to the world than meets the scientific eye, Mother insisted. She even looked at the history of science as the history of acts of faith. Not only did the hunger to know God and discover God's nature fuel and fire the scientific pursuits of Copernicus, Kepler, Galileo, Newton, and Leibniz (this was the theme of my senior thesis in high school), but the truth of scientific theories also is no more "provable" than the truth of scriptural statements, as Mother constantly insisted. In my graduate-school reading of Thomas Kuhn, Fred Polak, and Michael Polanyi, I would learn how right she was. For example, the assertion that "the sun will rise tomorrow" is suspect on a couple of counts. First, the sun doesn't "rise," which evidences how science uses metaphors just as generously as religion does. Second, the *petitio principii* argument—that the way things have always been means they will always be—cannot be logically justified and is easily falsified.

Mother didn't like evolutionary theory, but she didn't make a big deal of it. God could create any way God chose. I once asked Mother, "What if they find intelligent life on another planet? Will they need to be saved?" She replied without hesitation that God would send them Jesus, although with a different plan of salvation than ours, one that was compliant with their planetary culture and context. I found this to be one of the most liberating things she ever said.

Mother had an almost Jonathan Edwards–like sense of everything around her as alive: that God diffuses divinity in nature, even in something as seemingly inert as rocks. "Nothing," Edwards said, is "the same that the sleeping rocks dream of."[3] Even though we lived on a blighted street of a small industrial city, on a lot so small that only one tree grew on it, our daily existence never drifted far from an intimacy with the natural world, all the while retaining a rock-steady focus on our unique individual natures as children of God. In our little home, there was always a zooish assortment of birds (parakeets), cats, dogs, hamsters, turtles, colored Easter chicks that turned into swans, and even a crocodile.

Mother's green thumb could make anything grow, including a certain cactus in the backyard that my brother shot a giant hole in the heart of with his BB gun but that she still kept alive, partly because she sang to it, as she did with all her plants. She practiced wild digging before it had a name, and she found a rare, protected, and endangered jack-in-the-pulpit in the woods and transplanted it into the shadiest nook in our backyard. Visitors were forced to make pilgrimages to be blessed by this outdoor preacher.

My brothers and I were "free-range" kids. We were often shooed out of the house and sent exploring in Myers Park, a city park and recreation center past our elementary school

(Park Terrace). Myers Park was our Sherwood Forest. We went hiking in the woods and skiing on the back trails; we played tag in the fountains, sat like royalty in the king and queen chair, fantasized about being rock stars in the bandstand gazebo, and generally got lost in nature until we were due home for supper. Woe betide us if we were late, since we were the ones assigned to set the supper table.

Mother would have nothing to do with the notion of God speaking in "two books," the book of Scripture and the book of nature. There was only one book of revelation. The laws of nature were vacuous of virtues or values. The ways and means of nature don't care, while the ways and means of God care deeply.

Psalm 121 was to the evangelical world what a St. Christopher statue was to the Catholics. Every trip in the car began with a recital of Psalm 121. It was one of the earliest psalms I remember memorizing as a whole psalm (Psalm 1 was the other). The psalm begins with the following words:

> I will lift up my eyes to the hills—
> From whence comes my help?
> My help *comes* from the LORD,
> Who made heaven and earth. (NKJV)

Mother liked to point out that we are invited to "lift up our eyes" to the mountains, but only in order to look beyond the hills to the horizons of the heavens. That's where our help comes from: not from beholding nature but from beyond the hills where God reigns in the heavens. We lift up our eyes to the hills so we can see beyond the hills. The Creator is greater than the creation: "The heavens, even the highest heavens, cannot contain you. How much less this temple I have built!"[4]

We were never allowed to forget how many events in the Bible happened on hills: Mounts Moriah, Sinai, and Horeb; Galilee; the Temple Mount in Jerusalem; and Golgotha. On the mountain are events of deep passion: the sacrifice of Isaac, the Crucifixion. On the mountain are events of deep revelation: the giving of the Law, the Ten Commandments, the Transfiguration. On the mountain are events of deep teaching: the statutes of the covenant, the Sermon on the Mount. On the mountain are events of deep encounter: Elijah the prophet, who revealed the face of God to the people and encountered the presence of God on Mount Horeb as he was fleeing Israel.[5]

It was on the mountain that God and humans interacted in special ways.

It was on the mountain that the ark came to rest and Noah and his family came out.

It was on the mountain that God tested Abraham and Solomon later built his Temple.

It was on the mountain that Moses received the Ten Commandments.

It was on the mountain that Elijah had a showdown with the prophets of Baal.

It was on the mountain that Jesus and his disciples met with Moses and Elijah.

It was on the mount called Calvary that Jesus was nailed to the cross and saved the world.

It was on the Mount of Olives that Jesus would ascend to the heavens.

All mountain experiences are encounters with God that showcase God's proximity and holiness. In fact, at the giving of the Law at Sinai, the mountain was so holy that the people were forbidden to touch it, lest they die.[6]

We grew up as "urban Appalachians," although not in hotbeds of Appalachian culture such as Cincinnati, Pittsburgh, Baltimore, or Charleston—the great centers of Appalachian cultural and political activity that resulted from the "great migration" of the 1950s, 1960s, and 1970s. You can tell you're living in "urban Appalachia" by the traffic jams on Friday evening as mountain folk leave "yankees" and "city slickers" behind (Appalachians come up with their own slurs) and head for mountains that range from southern New York to northern Alabama. Mother spent the last eleven years of her life with me in the second-most important center of Appalachian culture: Dayton, Ohio, one of two "Kentucky cities" (Cincinnati is the other; Columbus, Cleveland, and Akron are known as "West Virginia cities").

The Sweet family participated in these hegiras to the hills on a regular basis. It was my job to pack the car until we were bursting at the windows so that when my father came home from work (preferably in early afternoon), we could "head for the hills" and arrive at the family homestead before midnight.

There were two unpredictables for every trip—first, my father's inability to pass a historic marker without stopping and taking a picture of it. But since we always took the same route to the mountains, over time we stopped for all the hallmarked signs; so for much of my growing up, we were not delayed on the outgoing leg of the trip.

The trip home was another matter. Just as Dad never saw a historic marker he ignored, so Mother never saw an interesting rock by the side of the road that didn't deserve a slam on the brakes. No matter who was driving, the car would be pulled over to the shoulder, and she would get out and muscle the rock (or when we got old enough, we would) into the car. The rock became a valuable sixth passenger in an already crammed vehicle. Every trip to the homeland was a version of the Lucille Ball–Desi Arnaz film *The Long, Long Trailer*—except that the Sweet family did it without the trailer.

The rest of the ride home, Mother would think out loud about where she would put the rock—inside or outside the house. For a family too poor (not "food insecure," but poor) to purchase any art, Mother's rocks were the closest we came to fine art. Like those sand artists of eastern and southern Africa, whose rock paintings constitute the longest enduring art form in the world and who practiced their craft from 28,000 BC to the nineteenth century AD, Mother believed every rock was God's artwork. It became the Sweet family's responsibility to frame that divine art properly. Mother was proud of the rock wall she crafted in the front of our house, and she could recall the provenance of each rock to anyone who showed an interest in her artwork.

In that framing of nature, we learned some things of significance. First, Jesus was probably a stonemason who learned his craft from his father Joseph. That's one reason Jesus loved stone stories and rock metaphors. These metaphors were anything but simple. Peter was the rock on which Jesus built his church, but Peter was prone to teeter on the rocks—he was a rock that fell, faltered, shifted, and failed. Christ the "solid rock" moved to those on the rocks. Jesus offered sweet honey from the rock[7] and rock salt that only came broken down into fine granules.

Second, creation is not some "means" that humans use and exploit to a greater "end." God created nature as an intrinsic good to be valued in and for itself—even rocks. British literary theorist Terry Eagleton—perhaps the best critic of "new atheists" like Richard Dawkins and Christopher Hitchens, who believe that Lady Luck or Mother Nature has always been in charge—contends that God created the world "out of love, not need."

> God the Creator is . . . an artist, and an aesthete to
> boot, who made the world with no functional end
> in view but simply for the love and delight of it. . . .
> The Creation is the original *acte gratuit*. . . . The
> world is not the inevitable culmination of some
> prior process, the upshot of some inexorable chain
> of cause and effect.[8]

The Promethean attitude to nature is to undress her and take her secrets by force, limb by limb if need be. The Orphic attitude to nature is to learn her harmonies and dance to her rhythms so that she will give up her mysteries from alignment and respect. Theologians tend to be more Promethean in undressing God and Orphic in addressing nature. Scientists tend to be Promethean in both, although some scientists, such as Leonardo da Vinci, were both Orphic and Promethean. Mother was Orphic toward both God and nature.

But Mother was also able to dream in two languages. On the one hand, she sang with passion, "This world is not my home, I'm just a-passin' through." On the other hand, she sang with all her heart, "This is my Father's world." The B-I-B-L-E was an acronym for "Basic Instructions Before Leaving Earth," and at the same time it was an acronym for "Basic Instructions for Building Life on Earth." The power is in the double vision, the binocularity, of a human being full of hopes and dreams and deeds for a different world, and of a world in which we are of only passing significance. The world is our home, and the world is not our home. Our mission is to make the world habitable for everyone until Jesus makes the world a heavenly home.

It is easy to make fun of the promise of some "pie in the sky in the sweet by-and-by." For those who never eat a full meal or who have little wherewithal to make sweet pies, "pie in the sky" is better than no pie at all. Hope that floats off in some "pie in the sky" always eventually drills down to earth.

Although we waited for Jesus to return at any moment and were warned that death could come when we least expected it, Mother never declassed this world as a dressing room for the Rapture or a green room for the hereafter. Heaven took precedence over the world, but if Jesus loved the world enough to die for it, so should we.

Mother was fully "in" this world but firmly "of" another world. Her heart was in heaven, but her home was on earth. She never formulated this in terms of "dual citizenship." But that's what it was. The Good News is a redemption story about a new heaven and a new earth. The birth of Jesus let heaven and nature sing a song of joy to the world. The promise of Jesus is an earth where thorns do not infest the ground, where "I am with you always, even unto the end of the world."[9] The death and resurrection of Jesus is a down payment on a world where, in the words of the last line of the John Ireland cantata "These Things Shall Be,"

*New arts shall bloom of loftier mould,*
*And mightier music thrill the skies,*
*When every life a song shall be*
*When all the earth is paradise.*

For Jesus, the earth is a heaven, literally his "heaven on earth." The world was of more than worldly significance. God has designed us to be creators—not co-creators but continuous sub-creators dedicated to perpetuating God's creative activity in the world. We need an otherworldliness that is not apocalyptic or escapist and a this-worldliness that is not utopian or hedonist. God's Story doesn't end with a church but with a garden city.

---

*Some fight over a foot of land here and jeopardize their hope of inheritance to the whole world. The Bible says "the meek shall inherit the earth," not inherit the heavens.*

MABEL BOGGS SWEET,
15 MAY 1957

---

Mother never could see how you could follow Jesus and not care for creation:

The heavens declare the glory of God;
And the firmament shows His handiwork.
Day unto day utters speech,
And night unto night reveals knowledge.[10]

Mother had no use for environmentalists who see humans as a pimple on the planet and not as a pearl in God's planetary oyster. She was horrified by the human treatment of God's creation, and she marveled how, given our fishing practices, there were any fish left in the ocean at all. The drift nets were the Dachau and Auschwitz of the sea. But she would be equally horrified today to see a case being made for the equivalent value of a silverback gorilla and a five-year-old child, or Bolivia's 2010 passage of a "Law of Mother Earth," which grants nature equal rights with humans. She would applaud an environmental bill of rights, but not one giving the earth "human" rights.

Creation is creative—and unfinished. When the Bible says that all creation groans,[11] it means that creation itself felt Judas's betrayal, creation itself took the nails, suffered the blows, and drank the hyssop.

The church's horizons are wrongly limited to the human world in the redemption story (Romans 8:19-23). Jesus' redemption returns harmony and beauty to creation: "The wolf also shall dwell with the lamb, and the leopard shall lie down with the kid."[12] Christ covers everything in the cosmos in new birth so that the universe—all in heaven and on earth—might be brought into unity in Christ.[13] The new community in Christ breaks down all barriers—cultural, economic, social, and ecological.[14]

# 4

# THE DREADED FOUR-WAY

*Radioactive fallouts? We need and are promised
through the Holy Spirit, Holy Spirit fallouts.
We hear of radioactive fallouts. If this, then the late
hour requires fallouts by the Spirit, as happened to
Paul. Where are our Holy Ghost fallouts?*

MABEL BOGGS SWEET,
24 APRIL 1959

As a child, I didn't have a tractable nature.

But that didn't stop my parents. In the world of birds and dinosaurs, it is often the father who teaches the kids how to sing, but I learned how to sing from my mother. It was my father, however, who encouraged me the most to sing my own song, and to do so with personal responsibility and individual accountability.

"Mom," I would say, "*they* can do this. *They* can do that."

"Yes, I'm sure they can. But you are not a Jackson. You are not a Schmimo. *You* are a *Sweet*. And I don't care where we live and on what street you are raised. *You* will not act that way. This home has a higher moral standard than that of the street."

When we were able to walk, Mother would dress us up in our Sunday best and have us walk down the street to meet Dad coming home from work. The Sweet kids' procession up and down the hill holding Dad's hand was her way of "evangelizing" the wretched corner of town where we lived with the witness of at least one family that was not succumbing to the garb and lingo of the "hood."

In the Sweet home, prayer, love, and the rod were a holy trinity. They went hand in hand. The "rod" went in the right hand; it was made of four leather straps and called "the Four-Way." Often ominously worn around Mother's neck, she kidded that it was engraved with the words "I need thee every hour."

Ancients believed it was possible to kill someone with a glance. Mother had a glance that could kill. But sometimes a glance was not enough.

We grew up in a town that made leather gloves (Gloversville), so there was lots of leather to keep the Four-Way fresh. I can remember only a few times when this instrument was used to thrash trash out of me. But when repeated attempts at "drumming" home a message failed, Mother took to "drilling" certain things into my brothers and me. She put it like this: A parent "writes" a life as surely as an author "writes" a book. Our woodshed relearnings took place, as it was explained to us, not "because you do not know the truth, but because you do know it" and choose not to live it.[1]

---

*Heavenly Father,*
*Discipline is so needful but*
*You are so faithful.*
MABEL BOGGS SWEET,
20 JANUARY 1957

---

It was a fundamental tenet in the Sweet household that success in life comes less from innate "gifts" or socio-economic "lifts" than from ingrained "grit." When it came to public education, Mother saw all aptitude tests as over-rated markers of success; she refused to allow me to skip some grades in school as a result of such "tests" because she felt I didn't have the passion to match any alleged potential.

Mother and Dad also announced that all three of us boys would be without any economic "lifts" to pay for college. College wasn't optional, but parental help paying for it wasn't possible. The only option was what initiative the three of us would take to make college a viable option. Self-mastery was the only route to self-fulfillment.

The self-discipline and deferred gratification instilled in

us cannot be overemphasized. It ramified into every corner of life, even the manual hair clipper Mother used to cut our hair—the one that pulled out as many hairs as it cut. Ordinary scissors would have done a better job and caused less pain. But she was teaching us "grit" and "grin-and-bear-it" determination. It was the same with how she washed our hair, massaging our heads (or more accurately, manhandling our scalps) with "Glover's Mange Cure," a foul, tar-smelling shampoo meant for animals.

Mother broke down the word *discipleship* into its component parts and took each part with utmost seriousness. You might say she put the word *discipline* back into discipleship. For a healthy life of faith, there was a required daily hygiene, a daily regime and regimen of disciplines and tools that dealt with the problem of human suckitude.

True passions are not those we first feel—-that's called sensationalism. True passions are those we discipline and test. The "testing" could occur when we least expected it. After Jesus defeated Satan in the desert, Satan didn't withdraw and leave Jesus alone. He slunk away "until an opportune time."[2] Such "times" reappear again and again. And the "times" when we are most vulnerable are not at the point of our weaknesses but at the point of our strengths—which is why subjection of the self for Mother was so important, and self-absorption so dangerous. Your truest and highest self is found in service and self-sacrifice, not in the satisfying of the self's desires.

*I am not my child's Savior. I am its Mother. I care for them in provision, precept, patience and protection. Save they find Jesus, I am just their channel to be born.*

MABEL BOGGS SWEET

God is not there to be used but to be obeyed.

God does not bow before our needs. We bow before God in surrender.

God is for us and with us, but God is also there to contradict us and convict us.

God is the crossing of the transcendent and immanent, the vertical and horizontal. The church gets in trouble when it uncrosses the two and focuses on one more than the other.

Each one of us found ways to "test" ourselves and exercise our self-discipline. My way of living Augustine's prayer—"To my God a heart of flame, / To my fellow-men a heart of love, / To myself a heart of steel"—was to never eat a cupcake or piece of candy at school. When parents would send pans of cupcakes to pass out at school for their children's birthdays, I would always hide mine, pretending I had eaten it, and then bring it home for my brothers and parents to enjoy. I learned that the gratification that comes from seeing others enjoy a gift is greater gratification than receiving a gift. The trip home—with the frosting intact at arrival—became part of the present.

*All the ingredients of cake are in a cabinet. But to produce a cake those ingredients must be measured and mixed. The gospel must be mixed with faith to produce a godly and Spirit-led life.*

MABEL BOGGS SWEET,
15 NOVEMBER 1957

There are gods—lots of gods—for sale, but God is not for sale. In the discipline of deferred gratification I learned that God traffics not in buy-and-sell but in give-and-receive; the only currency in God's economy is grace and mercy, love and forgiveness.

The problem with deferred gratification is that you can keep deferring in life until there is no gratification. This is not the Jesus way. In the Horatio Alger tradition, you waited to celebrate until you succeeded at something. Celebration was a reward for achievement. In the Jesus tradition, celebration is a style of life, a singing and dancing in the world, whether there is rain or sunshine.

～

Every person has faults, just as every mountain has crevasses. But we sons of Adam and daughters of Eve have a special design flaw: We refuse to bend at the knees for the divine, but we drop down and bow before every fad and fashion that pedestals the self.

Mother made it as hard as possible for the self to be the

center of the universe. God is our "all in all" (one of her favorite phrases). The self is in subjection to Christ and is constrained by the Scriptures. The self is not a demagogue that subjugates all external authorities to its will and whims. If we did not have the self-discipline to displace the self and defer our self-gratification, Mother would do it for us as long as she could.

My demons didn't come in a bottle or in tabs; they came on a card table or in a one-armed bandit. Mother gave great voice and ventilation to the belief that games of chance and card games preyed on the weak and vulnerable and targeted the poor. I don't know where I would be today if we had not been disciplined for playing cards other than "Old Maid." Mother never used physical punishment on us for card-playing, but the threat was always there: "You shuffle and I cut."

---

*A sad day. Feeling so keenly Lenny's desire to go to a dance. Word, "Stand Strong." "We shall be like a tree planted by the Rivers of Water" (Ps. 1). "Stand fast in the Lord." Demons have to be rebuked.*

MABEL BOGGS SWEET,
JOURNAL ENTRY ON MY BIRTHDAY, 14 MAY

---

*I have been working with problem and not with child.*
JOURNAL ENTRY OF "REVELATION"
A COUPLE OF DAYS LATER

If we heard it once, we heard it a hundred times—the story of four men who took a trip through the woods. Suddenly they came upon a high wall. Intrigued, they built a ladder in order to see what was on the other side. The first man to reach the top cried out with delight at the vision below and immediately plunged in. The second man did the same. And the third. Finally, the fourth man looked down on the inspiring scene: lush, green gardens as far as the eye could see and beautiful trees bearing every sort of delectable fruit. Never before had he beheld such a sight. Like the others, he started to jump right in. But as he paused for a moment to think of his family and friends, he decided to resist the temptation. Then he rushed back down the ladder and set out to preach the glad tidings of the beautiful garden to others. Each of the first three men had seen a new land of wonderful promise and decided to keep it to himself. One man deferred his gratification and sacrificed his own satisfaction for service to others.

---

*Everywhere I look I feel the need and urgency of His coming.*
MABEL BOGGS SWEET

---

It was the greatest fear of my life growing up. The fear kicked in when I came home from school, Mother was not there, and I didn't know where she was. As good pre-trib premillennialists, my brothers and I were taught that Jesus could return at any moment and that we had better be living a life worthy of being caught up in the air.

There was no doubt in anyone's mind that Mother would be swept up to meet Jesus in the clouds. There was some doubt about my father, since my brothers and I knew he liked to sneak out to see movies and we knew about the secret drawer in his rolltop desk where he hid racy military magazines. There was no doubt in my mind that my brothers would be left behind, since I knew what they were really like. Whether or not I would be left behind depended on whether or not the Rapture took place on one of my "good" days or one of my "bad" days—and the older I got, the more rebellion rushed through my veins and the more "bad" days I seemed to have.

My fear of being left behind was heightened by the fact that I was the oldest. That meant I would be responsible for my brothers during the Tribulation. Satan would be unleashed, persecution would become rampant, the mark of the beast would be burned on bodies, and I would be in charge of taking care of my brothers.

One day I came home from school, and Mother was nowhere to be found. I decided that my worst fear had come true. I have no idea what made me think this was R-Day. Maybe it was because the person I called (Ruth Kuhn) after the pressure built up didn't answer the phone. Whatever my reasoning, I believed I had been left behind. Mother had been raptured. Dad was at work and, as always, inaccessible. And at eight years of age, whether I liked it or not, I was now in charge.

What does an eight-year-old do who's trying to be responsible? Squirrel away food. We all had to eat, and who knew how long there would still be food on store shelves? So I gathered my brothers together, raided the bowl where Mother had been saving up money for some Robert Hall suits for the three of us, and hurried down the hill to Bowman's Market, the corner store a couple of blocks from our house. I knew exactly what food we needed to get us through the trying times ahead: a bottle of Quality Dairy milk, a large bag of chocolate chip cookies (Keebler, of course), and some food for the animals.

By the time we arrived back at the house with our survivalist stash, Mother had returned . . . and was frantic about finding her home empty of children. When I adultly explained that we had been to the store to stock up on supplies and admitted the source of the funds used for the purchase, she broke out the Four-Way. She allowed no defense, no excuse, but lectured me severely for my wastefulness and lack of self-control.

---

*We should be as concerned about sin,*
*as if we had a cancer.*
MABEL BOGGS SWEET

---

What came next was always the same. One of the biggest oxymorons of my growing up was the menacing "You do that and I'll give you a good horse-whipping." The "horse-whipping" I recognized as inherited Appalachian hyperbole, but in my young mind a "good horse-whipping" was a paradox. How could a spanking be "good"? In fact, when my mother prepped her "lectures" (such as this one on "wastefulness and watchfulness") with the ritual "this will hurt me more than it will hurt you" speech, I used to say, "Can't you just give me the spanking and spare me the lecture?" If Augustine's definition of preaching as an "audible sacrament" is true, the sermon that preceded the punishment was not a "sacrament" I wanted to take.

The Rapture incident was the first time in my life where I went from a position of "entrusting" myself to "trusting" myself to Mother. To trust someone is to believe they will not let you down; you have confidence in them. To entrust yourself to another is to put your life into their hands, to have enough faith in their trustworthiness that you bet your life on them. In the biggest crisis of my short life, I realized that Mother wasn't perfect, and she didn't always put my interests first. After this Four-Way treatment, I still trusted Mother. But I no longer entrusted my life to her.

# 5

# THE FAMILY BIBLE
# AT FAMILY PRAYER

*We do not gather every morning to advance an agenda or to
keep some ritual but to blast through Scripture and prayer the
hindrances that keep Christ from having control of our lives.*

MABEL BOGGS SWEET,

20 JUNE 1957

*Television tubes are conduits for power. The spiritual tubes of
prayer, Bible study and song, will reproduce the image of Christ in
our lives as effectively as television reproduces images on the screen.*

MABEL BOGGS SWEET, 19 JANUARY 1957

The name given to the routine of living in a religious
community is *horarium* (Latin for "hours"). Our home
was a religious community, and we had a daily *horarium*
built around something called "family prayer," which was
built around the "family Bible."

The family Bible was the closest we came to a castle. We lived in a tiny two-story house on a postage-stamp lot on a street called Hungry Hill. Mother ruled her little roost with a biblical grip. Faith was as much if not more a family matter than a church matter.

There is no more "evocative object"[1] for the Christian than the Bible. And the "family Bible" is the castle of Bibles, a moated palace in locked metal clasps and carved wooden bindings. These elaborate and hefty books, kept in "parson's cupboards" in the eighteenth and nineteenth centuries to be brought out when the parson came calling, hearken back to the first eleven hundred years of the church, when it was hard to read or even get a Bible.

For much of Christian history, the Bible was inaccessible to the common person. It was handwritten in Latin on parchment and cloistered behind the walls of monasteries and cathedrals. Whole Bibles were rare because illuminated manuscripts were too huge to be bound into one volume. A shivering monk in his *scriptorium* (cell) could spend his entire life transcribing and illustrating one book of the Bible (most likely a Gospel).

More readily available were Bible portions such as the Lindisfarne Gospels, one of the most prized and beautiful artistic creations of Western civilization. Created thirteen hundred years ago under mysterious circumstances, no page of the Lindisfarne Gospels is allowed by the British Library to be exposed more than once in five years or for more than three months at a time, and it must be always in subdued light.

*I read the Bible not because of habit or for merit
but because of my deep need of its strength.*
MABEL BOGGS SWEET

The Sweet family Bible was of humbler origin, a mass-marketed A. J. Holman heirloom with not even a personalized "Sweet" or "Boggs" on the front. My father bought one because other members of the family on both sides were in possession of the more pedigreed family Bibles. But he wouldn't pay extra for the name engraving on the cover.

The Sweet family Bible was reserved for special occasions such as Easter and Christmas. Mother, however, had her own leather-bound Bible for everyday use. She would get up early to pray and read so that the Lord could prepare her for the day's mission. She did not like to speak to anyone before her "walk in the Word," as she put it. My brothers and I would find her somewhere in the house with a cup of Sanka instant coffee in her hand, sometimes Noxzema facial cleanser on her face, and the open Bible on her lap—a Bible beautified by being battered, torn, dog-eared, graffitied, and stuffed with papers. Bibles that are falling apart belong to people who aren't.

"I arose early," Mother put it, "and met with God to work with me so I could work with them." "Them" was us. My brothers, Phil and John, and I were her three-boy mission.

*All sin is one sin: the worship of other than God.*
MABEL BOGGS SWEET

My enduring memory of Mother is not with one hand up in worship, but with one hand on her Bible. "They made me keeper of the vineyards, but my own vineyard I have not kept!"[2] This was Mother's way of talking (using King Solomon's words) about those who leave the fiddle at the door, or the shoes at the cobbler shop, or the Bible in the pulpit. Mother was never found in the house without the Bible by her side. It became almost an appendage to her body, something you expected to find with her at all times.

It was said that Benny Goodman never looked complete if he was not at least holding a clarinet and preferably blowing it; he was holding one when his fatal heart attack came on in 1986, when he was seventy-seven years old. Mother never looked complete if she was not at least holding the Bible, preferably teaching or preaching from it. She died in a hospital bed with a Bible in her hand.

When commanded to be a prophet, Ezekiel was given a scroll and told to eat it.[3] You speak to the house of Israel only after you've eaten the story. Scripture is to be internalized as the fiber of a person's identity and being, which is why Mother called her daily Bible study her "daily gleaning."

With apologies to Rudyard Kipling, Mother would not have understood the question "What do they know of Bible who only the Bible know?" She was convinced that everything everyone ever needed to know about anything was in this book. And everything in this book had you in mind. "This was written for us," Paul insisted.[4] The Bible is the church's book, the people's book, not the scholar's book: a book not just for "the learned" but for "the little ones." And she used it as her tool for child rearing.

It is the job of parents to embarrass their children, but Mother turned this job into a joke. She never met a stranger she didn't draw into a conversation, not about the weather or how the day was going but about her latest "word from the Lord." My brothers and I would find a way to slink away and hide when she was giving her *rhema* word.[5] Of course, if mother couldn't find someone to evangelize or enlighten, she always had us.

---

*The searchings of the Scripture should be that we may bear a stronger testimony of Christ, and not of just knowing the Scriptures.*
MABEL BOGGS SWEET, 22 FEBRUARY 1957

---

I learned very early in life how to go places in my mind while looking as if I were politely listening to my squirm-making mother descant on her latest word from the Lord. Later in life, I started to resent the fact that Jesus wasn't speaking to me as he was speaking to her, and this bitterness helped spark my adolescent deconversion. More than once, I threw the Bible across the room in disgust and dismissal. (By the way, the more likely you are to have thrown a Bible at someone or something as a kid, the more likely you are later to become a pastor. Often "Here I Am" comes after a "Leave Me Alone." At least that's the case with Noah, Abraham, Moses, Samuel, Isaiah, Jeremiah, Jonah . . .)

But one day I was gobsmacked by my dunderheadedness in not realizing that the very next thing out of Mother's mouth after "the Lord spoke to me" was a biblical passage. For her, the Bible was an accumulation not of lifeless facts and lists of numbers but of living stories and linked relationships that she lived daily. The place to find one's identity in life was in this storybook.

In graduate school I studied the parables of the Yiddish writer and Nobel laureate Isaac Bashevis Singer. A lot of my upbringing came into focus when I read these words from him: "If you read the Bible as just a good book, as poetry or prose or history, then you are not anymore a religious person."[6] Mother aimed to give her boys a storybook existence, but every story needs a script. In a world of make-it-up-for-yourself unscripted spiritualities, Mother insisted that the life of her boys be a scripturally scripted life.

Mother's interest in the Bible was not a scholarly one. Scholars of religion are interested in interpreting the Bible. Mother was a person of faith. People of faith are interested in interpreting life through the lens of the Bible. All of life, all words and all actions, are to be sieved through a biblical mesh. Or as Ma herself put it, "The Bible is my cross-reference." The Gospels in particular were not written merely to document the stories and sayings of a dead person but to convey what Jesus is doing and speaking today— a literary genre unlike any other. "Is our quest for knowledge and for understanding," Mabel Boggs Sweet preached to the congregation, "or is our quest for Christ?" Mother approached her daily "gleaning," or "hiding the Word in the heart,"[7] almost as a sacrament.

---

*The Holy Ghost is given that the Word may not become a Dead Sea but a river of flowing water.*

MABEL BOGGS SWEET

---

In spite of all the embarrassment as kids growing up, we got the sense that to be a follower of Jesus is to be heir to an extraordinary heritage, host to the very Son of God, and harbinger of a promised future. And the key to that heritage and hope was in this book. In fact, my brothers and I have often lamented how we received an indifferent education in everything that was not in the Bible—the classics, the sciences, the arts. Since imagination plays off what is available, who knows what we might have become if our minds had been thus stimulated?

Growing up in the families we are raised in makes us into the people we become. Hence, the "family" is often called the original department of health, education, and welfare. In our family dynamics, "HEW" headquarters was located in a time of "family prayer." Before we went to school and before we went to bed, family prayer was a nonnegotiable ritual of daily life. Long before Peter Ochs' landmark essay "Morning Prayer as Redemptive Thinking,"[8] Mother's mode of moral training was a daily liturgical formation based on oral readings of the Scripture and prayers in the morning so that you could make right judgments throughout the day. If I were asked to name the chief event in my life, I should say, "Family prayer."

The Sweet family knelt at "altars" twice a day (Mother gave up one heroic attempt at three times a day—"the biblical number"). These would last anywhere from fifteen minutes to an hour. Even as a kid, I realized that this was Mother's church, we were her congregation, and her "meditations" were her sermons. How my father fit into this I was never sure.

Dad was a pouter. I expected even then to find him pouting in Paradise. He always sat there dutifully, often more piteous than pious, as if he were one of the kids. When he called her occasionally "Mommy" rather than "Mabel," I never knew if this was for us or for him. When you live with a force of nature, you break if you can't bend with the wind.

---

*Read daily the Word. There is no merit in reading alone.*
*The power is in what you read and letting it work in you and read you.*

MABEL BOGGS SWEET,

20 MAY 1959

---

Family prayer began with one of us being assigned a portion of Scripture to read, from either the family Bible or another one of the many Bibles scattered in every corner of the house. The reading was always from the same translation. I was suckled and reared in the King James Bible. There are some things in life, such as the KJV for praying or the sacred bird (fried chicken) for eating, that could never be displaced in our household. I have a profound and ineradicable debt to the King James Bible.

The Bible reading was followed by a meditation from one of us (usually Mother) with a reflection on the text. Sometimes we would sing a hymn. But always the devotional rigamarole ended with everyone on their knees in a ring of prayer. These daily sonifications—the oral reading of the Scripture and praying out loud—meant that our souls were being shaped by biblical vibrations. And Mother was determined that her sons, no matter how lackluster their interest or lippy their irreverence, would be properly shaped for posterity.

More rebellious than my younger brothers, sometimes I felt like a one-man Greek chorus of dissent. The amount of energy this Sisyphean task drained from Mother daily I would never fully appreciate until I read her notebooks decades later.

---

*A very difficult day with Lenny. Pressed by him near to death.*
MABEL BOGGS SWEET, 13 APRIL 1965

---

The Bible was written for oral hearing, not silent reading. "Faith comes from hearing,"[9] the apostle Paul insisted, and the ears of faith (*akoe pisteos*)[10] are the primary organ of the soul. In the Sweet household the Bible was given a "close hearing" even more than a "close reading." Our faith formed ears to hear the Bible's stories sounded forth daily, the frequencies of truth fashioning "new creatures" in Christ. At family prayer the Sweet family became a monastic community: We aimed so to hear and sing the gospel that our lives would become a living Bible. My brothers and I were being put into the soil, in Mother's memorable metaphor, as "trees planted by streams of water."[11]

Heinrich Schliemann (1822–1890), the great German archaeologist who rediscovered Troy, was so mesmerized by the myths of ancient Greece that he "baptized" his two boys by laying a copy of the *Iliad* upon their heads and reading a couple hundred of Homer's hexameters aloud. In family devotions Mother was doing the same.

*What your mind feeds upon*
*is what your soul feeds upon.*
MABEL BOGGS SWEET,
REFLECTION ON MARK 7:20-23

What was most important to Mother was that "her boys" were being sonified in the Scriptures, that we would "say" and "sing" the Scriptures till they became the soundtrack of life. Beginning at age five, we had to deal with Mother's memorization requirement of a new Bible verse every day during the school year. My brother Phil puts the "Sweet boys predicament" like this: "As a child, I just wanted to play. But before I could play, I had to do my homework. But before I could do my homework, I had to practice the piano. And I couldn't practice the piano until I had learned my Bible verses."

When we were old enough to go to summer camp by ourselves, we were enrolled in Dr. N. A. Woychuk's Bible Memorization Association (BMA—now Scripture Memory Fellowship), where we memorized dozens of Bible verses a week for twelve weeks so we could attend Miracle Camp in Perth, New York (across the road from Healey's dance hall and bathhouse), for free. Every Friday afternoon, an outside "hearer" arrived at 28 Bloomingdale Avenue, and my brothers and I stood in front of her to recite the memorized verses we had been assigned that week. The Bible was something that we had to sound out properly—not just read or write but say. The sonification of the Scriptures was not an option.

---

*Lord, let your love in my heart help my mind to draw
from the Scriptures today what I need to serve you.*

MABEL BOGGS SWEET,
REFLECTION ON I PETER 3:18, 22

---

It's not that we could accuse Mother of hypocrisy: She practiced what she preached. Her Bible was an appendage of her body. A walking concordance, she seemed to know it as a surgeon knows a scalpel. She had a page in her Bible where she made entries of the dates when she finished reading through the Bible. She read through the New Testament two or three times as often as she read through the Old Testament. At least twice a year she read through the Old Testament and at least four times a year through the New Testament. For her these were not "books" but friends. These writers of the Bible were her conversation partners, her brothers and sisters in the cloud. When she finished one reading of James, she wrote this in her notebook: "James, I have enjoyed you. Someday we shall enjoy Jesus together."

Though she got enormously excited in the late 1970s over the news of Bob Dylan's conversion to Christianity, she never did understand his response when asked to nominate the most overrated and underrated books of the twentieth century: "Overrated and underrated: the Bible."[12] How could you ever overrate the Bible? The Bible was what enabled her as a child to deal with the fear of a panther chasing her and her sister while her parents and brothers were away, and what helped her to deal with the deaths of two siblings (Hallie and Margaret) and the burning of her house to the ground in the same year. "I couldn't live without my Bible," she would testify, while brandishing it like a firearm.

The notion that ritual incantation of KJV verses that no one understands will have meaning and power used to be called "magic." I call it "versitis." As someone who learned the Bible chapter by chapter, verse by verse, Mother had an acute case of versitis and passed that ailment on to her children. We all were less prone to behold the Bible as one, at once, in all its glory, and more prone to collect a vision of it: glimpse by glimpse, word by word (12,143 different English words, 8,674 different Hebrew words, 5,624 different Greek words—773,692 total words in the KJV), verse by verse, chapter by chapter, book by book, over years. The danger of versitis is that the Bible becomes all trees, no woods; all lumber, no landscape. This is why, for many Christians, the Bible has become like an old phone book: a whale of a cast but not much plot. (That's assuming we haven't lost the cast, too.)

In Mother's mind, the Bible was not flat. What it says in Leviticus is not of equal relevance to what it says in John. That does not mean that some parts are more important than others; all passages of Scripture are of equal value—but not of equal relevance. Some portions of Scripture applied to a culture that no longer existed.

Similarly, there was a huge difference between "truth" and "facts." We grew up hearing about the Scottish preacher (never named) who said, "Everything in the Bible is true, except for the facts." That's a pun and wordplay, of course, but Mother took it to mean that while there are facts in the Bible, it was not written as a book of facts. Cultures and contexts often determine what should or should not be considered "fact." The Bible was written not as a book of relative facts but absolute truths, divine truth communicated in stories, poetry, songs, prophecies, letters, histories, wisdom sayings, and apocalyptic literature.

What is the best translation of the Bible? NIV? NRSV? KJV? No, the best translation is the life that puts the story into daily practice, turning the Bible into the *living* Bible. If that is true, then my mother's Bible was the best translation I've ever read. She read her Bible in the Holy Spirit's language.

Mother could not understand bellicose biblicists who turned a missive into a missile and were prepared to fight to the death over what is more fact than truth. The Bible is our sword, but not a Texterminator that slays and smites. It is a surgeon's scalpel, a sword of the Spirit that heals and saves. The Bible keeps pumping out new meanings, not because the content changes but because the context changes in which the content is crucibled. The Good News is not new news but the old made new: deeper understandings of what was always there.

How the holy Hebrew Scriptures could become an "old testament" for some people was a mystery to Mother. She looked at Judaism as a complete religion and one that was under special dispensation. Jesus added nothing new, except to frame Judaism in the way it was meant to be and to become himself the Torah, making it possible to live the Ten Commandments not by knowing them but by knowing Jesus and living his life together.[13] How it was possible for Jews to be saved without a belief in Jesus Christ was a mystery of salvation beyond theological discussion.

When I later read how the Austrian Jewish philosopher Martin Buber called Jesus "my elder brother" and thanked him for causing over a billion Christians to read the Jewish Bible, I thought how similar that approach was to Mother's ability to see herself and her faith in a Jewish mirror. In her mind, it was actually more important for Christians to see through a Jewish lens than for Jews to see through a Christian lens, and Mother encouraged me to have Jewish friends and attend their bar mitzvahs, even though there were dancing and drinks there. My first taste of shrimp (which I told Mother about) and my first dance (which I didn't) was at the Jewish Community Center bar mitzvah of my friend Michael Schoenberg.

Mother was not a religious person. But Mother was a person of faith. In two ways Mother would have made a good Quaker.

First, like both the Society of Friends and Salvation Army, she had little use for specific sacraments but had a deeply sacramental view of life where the harmony between spirit and matter is seamless. Everywhere she looked she saw, to quote the catechism of the Church of England, "an outward and visible sign of an inward and spiritual grace."[14]

Members of the Pilgrim Holiness Church most often dedicated infants and baptized adults, but Mother always insisted I was "baptized," not "dedicated." She never could produce the certificate and never did understand my concern about the issue. "The whole world, in Christ, is God's 'sign,'" she would say.

The second way Mother's thinking resembled Quaker theology was in her clear demarcation between the Bible as the "word of God" and Jesus as the "Word of God." In fact, in her last Bible was a clipping of a George Fox quote: "The Scriptures are not the Word of God, but the Word of God is in the Scriptures." Another Quaker, Robert Barclay, put it a little differently: "The Scriptures are only a declaration of the fountain, not the fountain itself." You can't pin Christ to the cross or to the Scriptures like a frog to a dissecting table. All studies and searchings of Scripture were less about greater knowledge of the Bible and more about a stronger relationship with and testimony of Christ.

_____

*Some people know more about the Scriptures*
*than they do about the Christ.*
MABEL BOGGS SWEET

_____

Luke 1:44 says John "leaped" in praise in his mother's womb. How ironic that John the Baptist may have been the first closet "shouting Methodist." A die-hard and never-closeted "shouting Methodist," Mother accepted the Wesleyan quadrilateral. But Wesley's four sources of authority—Scripture, reason, experience, and tradition— were not a quaternity of equals. Scripture is primary. When the dead hand of rationalism holds Christianity in its stony grip, all energy and vitality—not to mention miracle and mystery—are drained out of it. Reason is a mentor, not a master—a guide, not a despot.

Mother never tried to figure out the Bible. She tried to figure out life from the vista of the Bible. Rather than try to reshape people's vision of the Bible and go from there, she started with a biblical vision. When I talked to her about Scripture and Creation as the "two Bibles" that reveal the divine to us, she reminded me that the star (nature) and the signs (culture) did not guide the magi all the way to Christ. They needed the Scriptures to go the rest of the way. To see Jesus, we need the Scriptures.

A feeling is not a fact. You can feel something without that feeling being based on any factual reality. A ditty attributed to Martin Luther is how we learned from Mother to "get it straight."

> *Feelings come and feelings go*
> *And feelings are deceiving*
> *Our warrant is the Word of God*
> *None else is worth believing.*

> *I'll trust in God's unchanging Word*
> *Till soul and body sever*
> *For though all things shall pass away*
> *HIS WORD SHALL STAND FOREVER!*

She never attributed this to Luther, only to "someone."

Every day, in one way or another, Mother taught her

three sons that "God's Word," the Holy Story, is the way that guides us, the truth that saves us, and the love that fills us. Mother was not guilty of bibliolatry—elevating the Bible above Christ[15]—but she was guilty of bibliomancy. She would never have owned an e-Bible; you can't open it up at random and plop your finger down on a Kindle verse. She practiced John Wesley's "at-random rule" and treated the Bible like any living organism: Anywhere will take you everywhere, since it's all connected. John Wesley practiced both sortilege (his term) and a systematic practice of Bible reading. This has led me to suspect that perhaps the ancient Athenians were right: Sortition (or the "lucky dip," a practice that chose the thirteenth apostle and is still how we choose people for jury duty) is a better way to choose legislators (local, state, federal) than the current "campaign" approach.

～

Much to everyone's amazement, Mother lived the last eleven years of her life with the one son who had given her the most trouble: me. When I accepted the presidency of United Theological Seminary in 1984, I moved Mother in with me as the First Lady to a house I had purchased partly with her in mind. It was an English Tudor a block from the seminary. Once owned by a physician, it had a side entrance for his office and a back stairs leading to a wing of the house with its own screened-in porch, dining room, living room, bedroom with fireplace, and bathroom. This became Mother's empire while she dealt with a declining heart.

Every Saturday night, Mother would sit by her phone with the Bible in her lap, waiting for the phone to ring. One of my friends, somewhere in the world, would invariably call her and ask, "Mrs. Sweet, what's the Lord spoken to you today?" For the next fifteen to twenty minutes, Mother would launch into her "word from the Lord" while they took notes for their Sunday sermon. I confess to many unsanctified thoughts about these calls. After all, Mother's words from the Lord rightfully belonged to me. After Mother died, my spirit didn't just go into a tailspin. My preaching took a nosedive as well. I had lost my enthusiasm.

The early Wesleyans were called "Enthusiasts." The word *enthusiasm* originally meant "God within"—the belief in God's power to occupy a person and speak through them. Mother didn't just look for burning bushes. She was one. She had become my throne room of "enthusiasm." I needed now to find my throne room within, not without. My prayer became a simple one, as I was drawn to John Wesley's purported response to why people came to hear him preach: "The Holy Spirit sets me on fire, and people come to watch me burn." I began to pray, "Jesus, the One who uses flames of fire as ministers (Hebrews 1:7), anoint my eyes to see, my ears to hear, my hands to touch, and my heart to feel until I can be your flame of fire."

# 6

# UPRIGHT PIANO AND SOUNDTRACK FOR THE SOUL

---

*God knows what God can do. God wants us to discover what we can do*
*if we yield our all to God. God is not going to do for us what we can do*
*for ourselves. The Director of a band plays no instrument in the parade.*
*He knows what he can do. But his job is to bring out the many parts*
*and players in one band to be their best and to make beautiful music.*
*God made worlds for us to play in, music for us to sing. But God*
*wants us to discover our need of His direction.*

MABEL BOGGS SWEET

Our home was inconceivable without music. Over our little house on Bloomingdale Avenue, there might as well have been these words carved in the doorpost: "Jesus, Susanna Wesley, and Johann Sebastian Bach Live Here."

In the Sweet household, if you breathed in the Bible, you breathed out music. The unstated assumption was that God's "word" yearned for and yielded—no, *demanded*—musical expression. One of Mother's favorite verses seemed to say precisely this: "Let the message of Christ dwell among you richly as you teach and admonish one another with all wisdom through psalms, hymns, and songs from the Spirit, singing to God with gratitude in your hearts."[1]

Music is to faith as air and water are to life. In the *Poetics*, Aristotle claimed that there were six constitutive parts to all dramatic arts that issue in "catharsis." We're familiar with the first five—plot, character, diction, thought, and spectacle—but we often forget the sixth: song, or music. Mother started with the sixth. Music and music-making move the world from *chronos* time to *kairos* time.

My brothers and I were not given a choice of whether we would be musical or not. To be a follower of Jesus meant you mastered one musical instrument beyond the piano. The only choice was which you would master. My brother Phil chose the guitar. My brother John chose the clarinet. I chose the bassoon.[2] Or more accurately, I chose brass; Mr. Clo, the band director, chose the bassoon for me. He needed a bassoonist, and I couldn't say no to Mr. Clo. I hated reeds, but I loved Mr. Clo.

The only thing worse than having to say, "I play the bassoon," would have been for me to say, "I play the triangle." I hated the bassoon almost as much as I hated the accordion, which was ruined for me forever by Lawrence Welk. No one has ever described an accordion better than a critic in the *Minneapolis Journal* of 16 December 1912, who called it "shameless" and "a fearful instrument that looks like a cash register, and sounds worse."[3] If I open my eyes when I die and see an accordion, I'll know I'm in the wrong place.

There was also no choice but that, as early as we were able, we would sing in public as part of Mother's entourage, which she dubbed "The Sweet Family." I supposedly started singing in public at nine months of age. We each had a signature song. My brother Philip's was "It Took a Miracle to Put the Stars in Place" (although I heard it as "It Took America to Put the Stars in Place"). John's song—"I Don't Have to Wait Until I'm Grown Up to Be What Jesus Wants Me to Be"—was especially annoying, less because of the song itself and more because of the piousness with which he sang it. My song was "Dare to Be a Daniel." The song we sang as a trio was "Peter, Peter, Peter, Peter on the Sea, Sea, Sea, Sea."

The church lives and dies on its stories and songs, its metaphors and music. That's why musicians are so important to the life of the church. A "song leader" or "worship leader" leads the music and song so that the Holy Spirit can "lead" the "worship." Musicians are priests, part of the priesthood of all believers. And what priests do is usher others into the presence of God, sometimes by the story and sometimes by the song.

It used to be that music was taught second in importance to theology, often by the same professor. There was a twinning of music and theology not just in worship but in study as well. That was the essence of our domestic dogma. Our early theological training was unrepentantly

Protestant, which meant that we were taught not to see faith as something found in tangible things, the way "those wafer-worshiping Catholics" did in their rosaries and prayer-books, ciboria and chalices. But the one celebration of the material world for us, besides the omnipresent Bible, was music and its songbooks, instruments, and accoutrements.

Mother took seriously the Henry Ward Beecher dictum: "What the mother sings to the cradle goes all the way down to the coffin." She began singing to us in the womb and continued throughout our childhood. When family prayer was over each night, my brothers and I would get up from our knees, give Mother and Dad a hug, and race each other upstairs to bed. Sometimes (always if we were sick) Mother would tuck us in physically. But mostly Mother would tuck us in musically: We would call down hymns we wanted her to play, and she would either play them by memory or look them up in one of the many hymnbooks scattered on the piano or stored inside the bench. If a radio pulls sound out of the air, prayer pulls sounds out of the heart. The assumption was that our musical requests would reflect the needs of our heart at that moment. There was hardly a problem that didn't have disharmony as its cause, and there was hardly a problem that a song couldn't cure.

Sometimes Mother would sing as she played. Sometimes she would hum. Sometimes she would only play. But sleep came with a soundtrack, played by cathedraled fingers that got thicker and more arthritic with every passing year. After Mother died, I purchased an eighteenth-century German upright piano made of pollarded oak, with the eagle symbolizing her favorite Gospel (John) hovering over middle C. Every time I walk past Mother's "indoor tombstone," I am reminded that music changes the world.

Our ramshackle upright piano took up much space in our living room, but not as much as Mrs. Busick's piano, where I sat every week to take lessons. When you opened the front door of her home, you negotiated a very proud grand piano demanding your respect.

The redeeming power of music to salve and save was conveyed by Alfred, Lord Tennyson in his "Charge of the Heavy Brigade at Balaclava" (1882): "The song that nerves a nation's heart / Is in itself a deed." Musical instruments in the Bible are weapons of holy war, able to bring down walls; as well as healing instruments, as in the hands of David before Saul and in the voices of Paul and Silas in prison. What have been the most important acts of worship in church history? Gathering at the table and singing, which somehow have gone together. Sharing of food and singing the story were features of our daily life as kids, just as singing at the table was a feature of the Lord's Supper.[4]

The child who remained awake the longest and proved the most needy for the therapeutic power of music would often be whispered back downstairs for one-on-one time with Mother and Dad. This is when we got to feel special, not just one of the three-boy pack. Often we were treated to ice cream or table time—upon strict conditions of secrecy.

Hymns are the best teachers of Scripture and the best

makers of identity: "Words of life and beauty / Teach me faith and duty."[5] If you asked people to recite Psalm 90, they couldn't do it. If you asked them to sing Isaac Watts' hymn "O God Our Help in Ages Past," which is Psalm 90 put to music, they could. Ditto "All People That on Earth Do Dwell" (Psalm 100). To "sing them over again to me"[6] is to etch deeper and deeper into the soul the doctrines of the faith. One of the greatest biblical scholars of the twentieth century, F. F. Bruce, was asked what books he would want with him on a desert island. Given the Bible and Shakespeare, what else would he like to have? Bruce replied, "Calvin's *Institutes* and Charles Wesley's *Hymns*. . . . The study of the *Institutes* would certainly keep the mind from going to seed, and Wesley's hymns would keep the soul from drying up."[7]

The received opinion—or at least the opinion I received—is that God likes a diversity of musical forms. All cultural forms are available to communicate the gospel, giving the church not just a freedom for diversity but an imperative of diversity. Very early in life I came to believe that the problem with Western Christianity was that there was not enough Africa or Brazil in it. Music has allowed Africa and Brazil a foot in the door, but it hasn't penetrated the theology or ecclesiology or liturgy. The more sophisticated a culture becomes, the more it needs to keep in touch with primary and primal feelings. Hence the importance of roots music. The life of faith is a journey in the taking, a project in the making, a story in the speaking, a table of bread in the breaking, a song in the shaking.

There are times when diversity is needed. There are times when solidarity is needed. Something my mother taught me as a child: "Lenny, if you ever get lost in a store, don't wander about. Stay in one place, and I will find you." A world that is constantly changing is looking for something stable and unchanging. That something is Jesus.

The gospel is not a set of timeless propositions but a timeless story that needs to be interpreted for every generation. The story of Jesus is more than our getting better at community relations, and his mission is more than social change. The story of Jesus is the solidarity around which dance many diversities.

The Christological basis to music was foremost in Mother's mind: "Let the word of Christ dwell in you abundantly."[8] "Abundance" also means "in a constantly new way." So here is another rendering of Colossians 3:16: "As the word of Christ indwells the members in the community and controls them, they teach and admonish one another in Spirit-inspired psalms, hymns, and songs." Admonishment and teaching were connected to "psalms, hymns, and spiritual songs," not just lectures and sermons and Bible studies.

This is why John Wesley captained a private campaign to popularize George Herbert's poetry, which I still love to this day. Great poetry made its way into my heart through songs. And in the wake of poetry came theology. Thomas

Aquinas was right: Both poetry and theology labor at the limits of language.

Rich spiritual practices go extinct just as species do. Classical music now accounts for less than 2 percent of recorded music sales in the United States, down from 20 percent in the early 1960s.[9] Solo singing off a screen is a very different musical experience from elbow-to-elbow hymnbook sharing, which I experienced growing up in churches with not enough hymnbooks to go around. You sang in parts and blended your voices with those around you. We no longer read songs, we read words—if we read at all. Music as a text is disappearing, replaced by sound documents supplemented by visual dramaturgy.

What has kept me from bolting out the back door of the church?

Certain books.

Certain people.

But most of all, certain songs, played on an old upright piano.

# 7

# POLIO BRACES

---

*Don't try to show off how much you know;*
*try to see how much you can learn.*

MABEL BOGGS SWEET

In a New Hampshire production of *Macbeth*, the line "Go, get him surgeons" was rendered "Go get him, surgeons." The biggest fights Mother got in were with surgeons and physicians.

To be sure, the women in the congregation of the local Pilgrim Holiness Church made it difficult for Mother. They resented what they perceived as her "immodesty" and "looseness" in wearing clothes that were too "fitting." (For Mother "modest" dress was an appearance that sought God's pleasure, not anyone else's.) They criticized her "boughten" and not self-sewn outfits. (Mother didn't like sewing.) At a time when this particular church viewed the piano as a dance-hall instrument, they attacked her piano playing. But most "worldly of all," she wore that infamous wedding band. It wasn't enough for these women that all camels must pass through the eye of the needle; it was their version of the needle through which all camels had to pass. This was the backdrop to one of Mother's favorite sayings: "You'll suffer as much from the church as for it."[1]

Vilified, reviled, and sentenced to hell, Mother even had some female "friends" curse the fruit of her womb when she was pregnant with my brother Phil. This proved tremendously upsetting to her—partly because she believed in curses; partly because, while she expected attacks from men, being cursed by women came as a surprise; and partly because she actually was pregnant. So this mountain girl, who was proud of her Appalachian ways and who enthusiastically nursed me and my youngest brother, John, was persuaded by Rosie-the-Riveter nurses in Nathan Littauer Hospital that the "modern" thing for an independent woman like her to do was to bottle-feed the fruit of her womb. The only one of us not breast-fed, Phil was the only one of us who got polio, "the emblematic disease of the middle twentieth century,"[2] when he was nine months old.

Mother had no way of knowing that before Jonas Salk introduced the polio vaccine, children were immunized against polio by actually playing in the dirt and grime and repelling the virus with immune support from mother's milk. The ghost of the women's curse and her capitulation to the "professionals" for bottle-feeding haunted Mother.

She told stories about this obsessively, almost one after the other, like old-fashioned sequential causality without the word *because*, for the rest of her life.

From as early as I can remember, Mother would rebuke our fuddy-duddiness about food with the words "You'll eat many bushels of dirt before you die." Dirt was our friend and something we needed. So she was even more fired up to fight for Phil against all comers because of her guilt over going against the grain of her "inner knowings," as she called intuition and conscience. She and my brother became, as he puts it, "loyal comrades-in-arms together in the polio war."

When Phil was in his early teens and 5'9" tall, an Albany orthopedic surgeon wanted to cut the muscles in his good leg to even out the length of his legs. The surgeon had done a series of articles on this type of surgery, and he warned my parents that without the surgery, Phil could be wearing shoe lifts of enormous sizes, which would destroy his hips. Mother asked how they could be sure his polio leg would stop growing.

"We know polio" was the response.

After much prayer and conversation, the answer seemed to come in the form of a question: "Why let a bad leg determine the future of a good leg?"

The Albany surgeons insisted that we trust them, as they knew what was best for polio patients. When Mother resisted this reasoning, they threatened to put my brother on a "do not see" list. The surgeon informed my parents that he would never treat Phil again, nor would any orthopedists in the upstate New York area. This turned out to be no mere threat: After my parents passed on the operation, my brother didn't see an orthopedist for over a dozen years. He was studying in Freiburg when his girlfriend (now his wife) convinced him to see a specialist, who outfitted him in his first "gauntlet" (a leather ankle brace). That brace enabled him for the first time as an adult to walk more or less normally. As it turned out, Phil grew to be my height, 6'4", and his polio leg grew with his good leg.

During Phil's repeated hospitalizations, Mother monitored his care when it wasn't common or kosher to look over the nurses' and doctors' shoulders. She fussed and complained to them that such-and-such wasn't being done right. I remember her many walks to the nurses' station to register the fact that no one had come to see him in a while, and her insistence that she knew everything about the medication, the casts, and the physical therapy being prescribed. She made herself such a nuisance that my brother got the best care in the whole ward.

Later in life, my father benefited from her constant monitoring of what was going on. At one point, doctors wanted to transfer my father from the hospital floor to a psych ward; he had started talking about the "Second Coming" and wanting to see Jesus in the air. When they announced to mother their diagnosis of paranoid schizophrenia, she insisted that her seminary son be told what they had told her. They refused at first but finally arranged to call me. When they explained my father's symptoms, which did seem a rather obsessive form of "Rapture readiness,"

I asked them how many pills Dad was taking. He was in the high teens of different medicines. Might his aggravated symptoms, I asked, have anything to do with the interaction of the meds he was on? I was told this was a complex area of "exponential medicine" and that they had no way of figuring out how one medicine might be interacting with another. I agreed to encourage Mother to allow Dad to be admitted to the psych ward—but only after they removed him from all meds and established a baseline, and then added back the meds one by one to see if this might have any effect on his symptoms. His hysteria disappeared after he was weaned from the cornucopia of pills. I never heard from the doctors again.

Mother insisted that we question all "priests" with fingers on the power levers and platforms of influence, whether they came wearing black bathrobes or white lab coats (or, increasingly, Food Network aprons). She likened the status of most people in "power" to that of Samson, with his locks shorn and his strength leaked out. He was without power "and he knew it not."

Mother loved to tell the story of the chair of a pastor-parish relations committee at a small rural congregation. He was very upset that the bishop had sent them a "female pastor," as he put it. He greeted her with a grunt and proceeded to make life miserable for her. Some of her colleagues suggested she take the old guy fishing, since that is one way that men seem to have bonded together for two thousand years. Well, the two of them got out on the lake and had just started fishing when the pastor realized she had left her jacket on the beach. She jumped out of the boat, walked across the water, retrieved her jacket, walked back across the lake, got into the boat, and resumed her fishing. After a long silence, the man spoke. "It's not enough they sent us a woman for a pastor. They sent us one who can't even swim."

In Luke's Gospel, the disciples dismissed the women's testimony about Jesus' resurrection as "idle tales."[3] Mother always insisted that this was a euphemism for "women talk"; men didn't believe women then, and they don't believe them now. So it was her role to, as she insisted (with a sparkle in her eye) were Jesus' words, "kick against the pricks."[4] It was the closest Mother ever came within our hearing to uttering a swear word, although I suspect, given how much more prickly the word has become, she would not have used it today.

Little sayings that Mother picked up from various places salted and peppered her everyday speech until the last days of her life, phrases such as "I've been told my place; I just refuse to go there." But she chose her battles carefully. When I was age nine I had my tonsils removed because it was the medical fashion of the day to look at tonsils as vestigial organs that were better out than in. Something happened during my surgery, however, to cause the surgeon to slip and cut out my uvula and part of my epiglottis. It left a gaping hole in the back of my mouth that totally changed my voice, my lungs, and my life. (One physician told me, later in life, "I can't believe you're still alive. Why haven't you choked to death?") There were spirited debates at our kitchen table whether it was the Christian thing to sue; it seemed that the physician who operated on me had a history of alcohol abuse that had led to other surgical "mistakes" and successful lawsuits. My parents finally decided that they could not maintain a Christian witness and drag someone through court, even someone who had grievously wronged their son.

In one way, this was the worst thing that could have happened to me. Besides the lifelong health consequences of this iatrogenic illness, I was known previously for the uniqueness of my voice, "a voice made in heaven." (I was a "miracle baby," left to die at birth as the medical team prioritized my mother's life after a difficult delivery. An off-duty nurse in street clothes saw a blue baby abandoned on the table and rushed in to rescue me. How my deliverance at birth had anything to do with the delivery of my voice was never made clear, but Mother was a pro at connecting strange dots.) My parents had assumed that I was anointed for a singing career—that is, if I didn't become a concert pianist instead, since I was publicly performing Bach, Beethoven, and Gershwin compositions that stumped pianists twice my age. But after the surgery created a cavernous crater in my mouth, I lost my singing voice and, slowly, my passion for music.

In another way, however, this surgical slip was the best thing that could have happened to me. I got all the ice cream I wanted during my long convalescence, thanks to a deal with the hospital. I was forced to find alternative passions (like sports and writing), which protected me from the disability of the "child prodigy" syndrome. In the words of

Leopold Godowsky, "When a child prodigy grows up, the prodigy vanishes and the child remains."[5]

Some people are born finding thorns among roses. Some people are born finding roses among thorns. We Sweets were born finding roses overrated and thorns in the flesh redemptive. We didn't seek out crosses to carry, but we didn't run from the crosses cast across our path, either. Everyone will have crosses to bear and one cross to die on. No one gets through life without afflictions. But in Christ, our affections can strengthen and sweeten through any affliction. The key to living a fulfilled life is to drink to the full the cup you are given. Jesus did not dilute his cup with painkillers or numbing plants. He drank it to the dregs. Suffering is not only a season or just a strange thing;[6] some suffering is a cup of special service that some are called to drink.

My two favorite woods—the woods I find most beautiful and engaging—are burled walnut and tiger maple. The first is created from an injury to the tree; the second is born of a disease. Something precious comes to us in such pangs and pains of life. Indeed, this preciousness comes to us only as we experience the negative as well as the positive for all they are worth. Jesus didn't give "it's not as bad as you think" comfort. He warned that it could be much worse than we think. But nothing can cut us off from God's love, and always underneath are the everlasting arms.

That said, while I love it when God is tender and caring with me, when God starts challenging and poking and provoking me—not so much.

# 8

# YELLOW CHEESE

*When will we ever get it—what matters isn't where you come from.*
*What matters is where you're going and who is traveling with you.*

MABEL BOGGS SWEET

There is American poor, and then there is Appalachian poor. Appalachian poor is more like African poor. In mountain culture we sang a lot about the "pie in the sky" because that was sometimes all there was to eat.

Our bread and butter were flights from reality. As a child I daydreamed of living in a house with a garage, a breezeway, a yard, a patio, and all the jam I ever wanted. As a teenager I dreamed of owning a Timex, with never a thought of a Rolex. As children we learned a weekly discipline of fasting. I used to think this was inspired by John Wesley, who often fasted from Thursday supper to Friday at 3 p.m. But after revisiting the street where I grew up, I suspected there was another reason: If we hadn't fasted once or twice a week, we'd have starved.

When Mother and Dad were not insisting on Sunday afternoon "naps," with everyone banished to the bedrooms for an hour, we took Sunday afternoon drives. I always asked to go look at the houses "where the rich people lived." So we would drive through fancy neighborhoods like Kingsboro Avenue, but our oohing and aahing about some beautiful estate would be beaten back with the bubble-piercing review "Some crook lives there." There was an assumption that wealth meant misbegotten gain; the wealth we were to accumulate was in heaven.

At the same time, paradoxically, there was an assumption that one day, if we lived right and worked hard, we could live in a house like that. It was a goes-without-saying assumption of our household that faith in God enhances mental and physical well-being, reduces criminal deviance, and promotes material wealth and "mansion building." There are many mansions in God's house. Don't live in someone else's mansion; build your own, the one God made you to build with your life.

But ultimately the Kingdom of God is not about things, and Jesus deplored the moral degeneracy of the rich, while at the same time warning the poor against envy. As much as my Appalachian ancestry denigrated the rich, there was also the recognition that the rich are important for all economic sectors. Scare away the rich and the middle class eventually becomes poor, and the poor become destitute.

Mother raised her three boys on the "wrong" side of town: a street in "Stump City" (Gloversville, New York) called "Hungry Hill" by the locals. Bloomingdale Avenue was the street's proper name, but all its residents were willy-nilly "ridge runners," so steep was the incline of the road. One kid our age built up such a head of steam going down the vertiginous street on his bike that, when it skidded on a slick, he was thrown to the curb and killed instantly.

Back in West Virginia we would have been called "trailer trash," one generation removed from the outhouse. In mountain culture, the richest people lived highest on the hill, and the lower you descended on the street, the lower your socioeconomic status. (This was exactly the opposite of the wider culture, where the best rooms in nineteenth-century European hotels and apartment buildings were on the second floor, while the servants or poor lived under the rafters and at the highest levels. All this changed with the invention of the elevator, which made the attic the penthouse.) We lived halfway up Hungry Hill.

Novelist Richard Russo's *Mohawk* and his Nobel Prize–winning *Empire Falls* provide good descriptions of the towns of upstate New York that the future left behind. Russo actually was born in Johnstown, but he moved to Gloversville (Johnstown's twin city) as a kid. Russo attended the parochial Bishop Burke High School, whereas I went to the public school.

Like Russo's grandfather, my grandfather Ira Sweet was a glove cutter. About 95 percent of the gloves made in the

United States up until the end of World War II were made in Gloversville. The glove industry began to decline at the end of the war as the fashion changed. But the greatest cause for the demise of Gloversville was outsourcing to Asia. The once-proud city of craftsmen began to receive "unfinished" gloves requiring only one button or one seam. This way the glove companies avoided tax and benefited from cheap labor.

Almost everyone on our street was on some form of government assistance. Except the Sweet family. We were too proud and too proper for that. Christians sell out their birthright when they get more focused on and excited about what government can do than on what God or the church can do. "We will not live by the sweat of other people's brows," my mother insisted. My parents would only accept "Godfare," not "welfare." My father's job as a bank teller required him to dress up in a suit and tie every day, a poor boy in a rich man's part (like Richard Nixon or Edward Heath).

For the people on our side of town, everything cost more and took more time. As James Baldwin put it, it's extremely expensive to be poor.[1] The rich get tax deductions; the poor get fees. Borrowing money and cashing checks cost more— sometimes 400 percent more. If you don't own a cell phone, one call on a coin-operated phone can equal the cost of a month's cell phone service. The trenches to put wires underground never were dug on our side of town; telephone poles drooped with hastily draped wires. The store at the end of our street was always open when we needed something in a hurry, but it charged prices that were twice as high as everywhere else. The only thing that didn't cost more was taxes: Poverty is a foolproof tax shelter.

The first use of the term "life stream" I have encountered came from a poem William Blake wrote to a patron about what it meant to be a starving artist. He wrote that he and his wife "eat little, we drink less."

> *This Earth breeds not our happiness.*
> *Another sun feeds our life's streams,*
> *We are not warmèd with thy beams.*[2]

As children we did not know how poor we were, partly because we were rich in everything that mattered and "another sun" fed our life streams. We were so under-privileged that we were overprivileged. Our house was a slum; our home was a heaven.

But we still needed to be fed, which is where I swallowed hard and did something that still makes me cringe.

Across the street lived multiple generations of one family in a house that looked a little like the dilapidated shoe-house of fairy tale fame. The house had a distinctive odor: a mix of alcohol, cigarettes, and other things I dared not ask about. Once a month, from as early as I could remember, Mother would send me over on a mission.

When none of our neighbors were looking, I would scoot across the street under cover of darkness, sneak around back, and knock on the rickety kitchen screen door. Mrs. Jones (obviously not her real name) would always greet me with a smile. I would always look up at her and say the same words: "Anything for the Sweet family?"

Sometimes she said, "Nothing this month." Sometimes she said, "Let me see what I have left over." And sometimes she had something ready and waiting. My arms would be filled with government surplus items—powdered eggs or bricks of yellow cheese.

To this day I shudder at the very thought of Velveeta and refuse to eat any cheese that's yellow.

I can tell you from personal experience about the philanthropy of the poor to the poor. The Sweet family gratuitously asked for and gratefully received the castoffs of society's castoffs. At Christmastide I love to sing of good King Wenceslas (907–935), Duke of Bohemia, who didn't send out end-of-the-year, tax-deductible charity checks but personally visited the poor in need, carrying his own logs. Too often we celebrate and venerate the poor rather than being in relationship with them. The Bible does not say, "I was hungry, and you feted me." It says, "I was hungry, and you fed me."[3] Gandhi said that this question needs to attend our choices: "What advantage does this decision you are making offer to the world's poorest?"[4] It's a question the poor are more likely to ask than the rich.

After fifty years of reading letters from people in need, Ann Landers famously said she learned this: "Poor wish to be rich, rich wish to be happy, single wish to be married, married wish to be dead." I laughed when I read this, but for Mother the laughter was misplaced.

Accumulation (of knowledge, power, wealth, security, piety, relationships, and the like) can be good. There are such things that are necessary components of human existence. But when the accumulation of one or more ingredient to the abundant life becomes tyrannical over us, then the good becomes an idol that destroys life rather than bringing life. As Paul puts it, we are prone to worship and serve the creature rather than the Creator. The "eternal power" of God is revealed through "what has been made."[5] But the ultimate in life is to trust not in things but in the intangible, unintelligible, incomprehensible, and eternal God. The elevation of the good, the true, and the beautiful to absolute status is the essence of idolatry. Idolatry is not evil made good. Idolatry is good made absolute.

In one of those Tennessee Williams plays that Mother would never let us read, a character argues that the greatest of all differences in this world is not between rich and poor or even between good and evil, but between those who have loved and those who have only watched with envy.[6]

# 9

# SWEET'S LINIMENT

*Jesus is the Great Physician. Anyone who feels he can study the*
*body without the faith and orders of the God that made it would*
*be like to study a building and not the blueprint or the architect.*

MABEL BOGGS SWEET

I come from a long line of healers on my father's side.
The irony was that Dad was totally disinterested in this
part of his heritage, while Mother was utterly fascinated
by it and did her best to pass it on. She mixed the herbs
and ingredients to the secret recipe that formed the famous
"Sweet's Liniment," and she distributed the healing elixir
free of charge to anyone who needed it.

Before there were physical therapists, osteopaths, and
chiropractors, there were bonesetters. For ten generations,
the Sweets practiced the healing art of bonesetting, which
was codified in 1843 with Waterman Sweet's first treatise
on the subject.

Bonesetter John Sweet came to Salem, Massachusetts, twelve years after the Pilgrims arrived in Plymouth. In 1638 he left Massachusetts to go to Rhode Island in support of Roger Williams, who had been banished from the Massachusetts colony because of his belief in the separation of church and state.[1] Bonesetting was one of the "professions" open to the sons of executioners, whose work was too "dirty" for their kids to become physicians or priests. Bonesetters mostly made their living by performing some artisanal craft; the healing art was a side business. Bonesetting was often the highest profession available to people in poverty. Professional bonesetters were known for pride in their craft and for mistrust of "professional medicine" and its horrendous standard procedures of bleeding, purging, and poisoning. Other than a couple of simple surgical procedures and the inoculation for smallpox that was discovered in the early 1800s, it wasn't until sulfonamide antibiotics arrived in the mid-1930s that a visit by a physician was likely to make you better or cure you.[2] Before antibiotics, "Cure seldom, relieve often, comfort always" was the physicians' motto. No wonder people like Lord Byron feared the doctors more than the diseases: "The lancet has killed more than the lance," he liked to say.

Bonesetters believed that you can be credentialed and adorned in a professional uniform and still be uninformed about how the body really works. A few bonesetters saw their healing as "supplemental" to professional medicine, but most saw their healing as "alternative." They practiced naturopathic medicine before there was a name for it. And they could set broken bones with an expertise that went far beyond most physicians. Bonesetters were opposed to the cold, rational, scientific approach to medicine that fails to recognize that many illnesses are not either psychological or physiological but rather a combination of both. Bonesetters were harbingers of the holistic medicine that abounds today.

Each generation of bonesetter Sweets passed on a secret recipe for an herbal remedy called "Sweet's Infallible Liniment." The recipe was passed on to me, along with a copy of the first edition of Waterman Sweet's first bonesetting textbook. I never thought I'd ever find an original bottle in which Sweet's Liniment was sold publicly during the mid-nineteenth century. Thanks to eBay, I found one.[3]

Mother believed that in prescribing Sweet's Liniment and passing it out, she was carrying on the Sweet bonesetting tradition and reminding the world that no matter how dire the predicament of the moment, "dem bones gonna rise again." She also believed she was continuing her own ministry, except under a healing cover. With the liniment always came one or more of the following sermons:

- You can open the door of every day with the handle of faith or the handle of fear.
- The power of the mind can influence our physical bodies: "As he thinketh in his heart, so is he."[4]

* You'll live a happier, healthier, more enlightened, and more adventurous life following Jesus than "following the world."

* Salvation is something done in us, not just for us; conversion is a personal transition from illusion to reality. (Mother didn't have the formal education to know this, but early Jewish and Christian writers translated *salvation* as health, or soundness of mind-body-spirit, or wholeness of being. William Tyndale translated the Bible from Greek to English for the first time, and when asked, "What is salvation?" he answered, "Health."[5])

* When troubled or in trouble, we often look to ourselves: what we are doing, what we have done, what we can do. Don't. Look to Jesus, what he is doing, what he has done, what he can do.[6] This is why Mother had little use for therapy or psychiatry or spiritual direction, which often tries to get us to "look inward" when Mother insisted we should "look to Christ." At one point Mother simultaneously mentored two women, Ethel and Mavery. The difference in working with the two of them, she said, was that Ethel wrestled with her problems, and Mavery wrestled with God.

* Jesus is medicine for life: "The Great Physician," Mother would preach, "will see you now." St. Jerome (347–420) described Luke, writer of Mother's second favorite Gospel, as "a physician of Antioch . . . not unskilled in the Greek language. An adherent of the

apostle Paul, and companion of all his journeying."[7] What we know about the early history of the church we learn from Luke and Acts, which St. Jerome said "acts as medicine for the ailing soul." The historian Eusebius (fourth century) wrote that Luke and Acts were two medical books to heal not our bodies but our souls.[8]

Mother was a committed Wesleyan, not just because she loved the hymns, Susanna, and the stories but because of the inclusiveness reflected in Charles Wesley's assertion that God looks on all of us, saved and unsaved alike, with "undistinguishing regard."[9] Jesus doesn't just hang with us when we're at our best or doing our best. Jesus stays with us, as he did with Judas, when we're at our worst. So whether you're at your best or your worst, Jesus is with you.

Jesus doesn't defend us from our past. Jesus demands that our past be turned over to him. If we give our past to him, he will take it, transfigure it, and turn it into something that can empower and embolden us without our needing to fear it or fight it.

Mother also loved John Wesley's fascination with physical health. His medical guide, *Primitive Physik: Or, an Easy and Natural Method of Curing Most Diseases* (1764), was a practical guide for those who couldn't afford doctors. There are also several accounts of supernatural healing in Wesley's journal. One of his friends, Mr. Meyrick, became sick and comatose. When Wesley went to check on him, Meyrick's pulse was gone. Wesley and several friends immediately prayed, and before their prayer was over, Meyrick's speech and sense had returned. Wesley wrote: "Let us examine the gift of healing. I have frequently said that it is not a sin to be sick or to die. It is, however, a sin for sickness and death to go unchallenged because there is no one to pray."[10]

---

*Sin is no problem to God. All that was taken
care of in Calvary and Resurrection.*

MABEL BOGGS SWEET

---

Just as Jewish mothers of the first century would sew a seamless garment and give it to their firstborn when he or she left to study at the Temple at age twelve, so mothers in the not-too-distant past would hand-wrap a package and give it to their firstborn son on his eighteenth birthday. The package would contain two long strips of percale material, which the son would recognize immediately as his mother's apron string. It was the most beautiful gift that any boy's mother could give him: The time had come to "let go," and no matter how much it hurt, no matter how much she might want to hang on a little longer, no matter how much he would forever be "my baby," the mother was untying the knot and surrendering this precious slice of her life.

Love cherishes the most when it lets the loved one go. When parents truly love a child, they give him or her away.

We give them away for baptism.
We give them away to kindergarten school.
We give them away to the school of hard knocks.
We give them away to college.
We give them away to a boyfriend or girlfriend.
We give them away to a husband or wife.
We give them away for life, to live their own lives.
We give them away for love.

Mother let me go when she gave me the secret formula for "Sweet's Liniment" and turned over to me the making of the medicine.

# 10

# LYE SOAP

———————— ❧ ————————

*There is no office so important that would justify us in*
*not fulfilling our responsibility to our children.*

MABEL BOGGS SWEET

M y Appalachian Gramma had washboard hands. My
mother had lye fingers—thick, swollen, stubby, and
manly. Both were proud symbols of the sacrifices made to
keep their families afloat.

To bring in a little money on the side, Mother sold hand-
made lye soap up and down the street. It didn't bring in
much, but every little bit helped. She viewed her lye fingers
and other sufferings as a sacrifice that made sacred the calling of raising "her boys." She picked out this passage from
Paul to summarize her attitude toward her children: "The
children ought not to lay up for the parents, but the parents

for the children. And I will very gladly spend and be spent for you; though the more abundantly I love you, the less I be loved."[1]

Three words were connected in Mother's mind: *sacrifice, suffering,* and *sacred.* She didn't know that the word *sacrifice* literally means "make sacred" (Latin *sacer* [sacred]; *facere* [make]). But she did know her Bible, where Paul says to make everything you do sacred, a "living sacrifice."[2] Jesus gave himself for our sins. Not money. Not jewels. Not property. Himself. It is giving of ourselves, the sacrifice of self, that brings deliverance.

In Mother's mind, it is the very definition of youth to be half-baked. Why? Youth haven't endured life's heat enough. They haven't suffered and sacrificed enough. "Suffering produces perseverance; perseverance, character; and character, hope."[3]

Mother spent almost twenty years in home missionary work and church planting. One of the stories my brothers and I liked her to tell was when she was invited home for Sunday dinner by a family high in the hollers of West Virginia. Mother had preached that morning, and part of her "payment" for preaching was to be fed by someone in the congregation. Mother's story wasn't as vivid as Catherine of Siena drinking pus, or Catherine of Genoa eating lice, or Angela of Foligno drinking water from sores of lepers, but it almost was. The home of the family hosting her was difficult to reach. They lived in a log cabin deep in the mountains. Sunday dinner consisted of some corn bread, hot out of the wood stove; some homemade apple butter; and a glass of milk. The problem was that the milk was peppered with flies—so thick with flies it looked like peppered mashed potatoes.

"What do you think I did?" my mother would ask my brothers and me rhetorically.

We groaned in grossed-out delight. "You gulped it all down!" This pepper-milk story is where we learned the "covered dish prayer": "Lord, make me equal to this opportunity."

Later I learned of a story about a father of three boys. The father was often gone on long trips. The mother taught the boys the importance of showing their father how much they had missed him when he came home. After one trip, the father collapsed in his recliner, and the oldest son, wondering what he could do, thought of getting the week's newspapers. He presented them to his dad, who gave him a big kiss and hug.

The middle child wondered what he could do and thought of getting his father's slippers. After he had put them on his feet, the father give his middle son a big kiss and a hug.

The youngest child couldn't think of what he could do. Then he went to his father and asked, "Dad, would you like a nice big glass of milk?"

"Sounds terrific," the father responded. He watched as his son walked very carefully, carrying the glass into the room, holding it so that four of his fingers were in the milk. Dirt from under the child's fingernails was making the white milk brown. By the time the milk got to him, the milk looked chocolaty.

The father took the milk from his youngest son, closed his eyes, and drank every drop. "That's the best glass of milk I've ever had."

Whenever I have been asked to eat uncomfortable food items around the world, I think of Mother's "pepper-milk" and the "covered dish prayer." And I gulp it all down.

~

But nothing is worse to drink than lye soap. Mother was not averse to employing the "wash your mouth out" threat, which of course her mother had used on her. Every word we spoke, from insults and cussing to boasts and blasphemies, entered the "ether wave," Mother insisted. They would haunt us eternally: "Every careless word that people speak, they shall give an accounting for it in the day of judgment."[4]

Those "ether waves," which go out into eternity, were Mother's way of handling Ecclesiastes 3:15, where God retrieves what is slipping away. She was convinced that Thomas Edison's end-of-life device to "read spoken words off the walls" would prove her right. Mother even bought us a boomerang to teach us the "principle of the boomerang," which today we would express as "what goes around comes around." My sassy response to "the boomerang principle" almost got me a mouth-washing: "But only if the boomerang doesn't hit its target."

Mother tried to get us not to swear by cracking the wash-your-mouth-out whip from behind and dangling the carrot from up front. We didn't want to be conformists, did we? Teenagers learned to swear, she argued, because they wanted to fit in with the crowd. We were supposed to be different, not fit some teenage cliché.

I got my mouth washed out only once—with Ivory soap, not lye soap. I didn't feel I deserved my punishment, since all I'd said was what I had heard my aunt Jean say about why she didn't visit someone's home: because their house was filthy and never cleaned. That was my first lesson in the meaning of discretion and the need sometimes to keep the volume low, to "think it, sink it, don't blink it."

The one time I deserved to get my mouth washed out with soap, I didn't. In sixth grade I was walking home from school with my friend Mark Otto and another classmate. Mark used a word I hadn't heard before. I asked him what it meant. He looked down the hill, about ten houses away, and saw my mother out front, sweeping the sidewalk. "Why don't you ask your mother?" he replied.

So I did. I yelled down the street, "Mother, what does the word *f---* mean?"

My friends cracked up in laughter. "I don't think she heard you!"

I yelled it louder. The more they laughed, the louder I yelled.

When I got home, Mother whisked me into the house. Realizing how badly I had been set up by my "friends," she bristled, not at me but at my friends for snookering me.

She used the incident as a teaching moment to warn me of being lured into danger by my desire to be popular.

The power of the human tongue is immeasurable. This smallest of organs, a toxic turbo tongue can easily cause more hurt and destruction than any other part of the human body. In fact, you can strike a person in the face with your tongue just as viciously as you can strike them in the face with your fist. People who play with fire are called pyromaniacs; so, too, are Christians who play with tongues of fire. And these verbal pyromaniacs can set ablaze whole buildings and whole movements just with their fiery tongues. When people ask me today, "Sweet, why are you so fond of new or made-up words?", I respond with Dennis Potter's well-known answer: "The trouble with words is that you never know whose mouth they've been in."

# 11

# MOUNDS, MARS BARS, AND
# THE COUNTY HOME

---

*People need to know that God is for them, not against them.*
MABEL BOGGS SWEET

From as early as I can remember, at least one Sunday afternoon a month, Mother carted my brothers and me to the Fulton County Home, also known as the "county farm" or "poor farm." There we conducted Sunday services for the residents. My brothers and I would perform our musical numbers, and Mother would preach, often ending her sermon by singing a solo and leading those present in the song.

My brothers and I loved to spend Sunday afternoon this way for a simple, selfish reason: We got candy. Not from Mother, of course; she seldom bought us candy because we couldn't afford such luxuries. But there was one toothless gentleman at the county home who, after the service was over, delighted in hobbling up to us on his cane, looking for a chat and bearing gifts. Each of us would get a Mounds bar, a Mars bar, or an Almond Joy. I fought or traded for the Almond Joy. We suspected he stashed away some of his treats and desserts just to have enough to give to "the Sweet boys." Once again, the generosity of the poor stands as one of the wonders of the world.

We always had to wear our "Sunday best" to these services. That meant dark suit, white shirt, and tie. Mother would dress up as if she were going to a formal concert. Sometimes she would let us wear something special, like a cowboy suit for my brother Phil, or a pirate suit for my brother John, or my Davy Crockett outfit.

One of my earliest memories was of the Davy Crockett frenzy. I managed to persuade my Aunt Patsy (who lived with us and worked at J. J. Newberry's at the time) to get me one of those 300 million coonskin caps that were sold. Crockett was the second-most famous man in America in his day (behind President Andrew Jackson), but Crockett opposed Jackson's 1830 Indian Removal Act, which legalized the expulsion of all "C" tribes (Cherokee, Choctaw, Chickasaw, Creek) from ancestral lands. Even though we were not allowed to watch the show because of the violence, I snuck peeks at Fess Parker playing Davy Crockett, "King of the Wild Frontier," as he and his buddies grappled with grizzly bears, wolves, and buffalo, not to mention Indians, Yankees, Missourians, and "Methodizers."

Crockett became my alter ego, especially the way he lionized horse sense and belittled book learning. It made me wonder later: Why is what John Calvin or John Wesley have to say about faith more important than what Mabel Boggs Sweet has to say? Wish I still had my coonskin cap today.

It took me decades to appreciate what Mother was doing in arranging for the Sweet family to take responsibility for Sunday worship at the county home. It was Mother's way of exposing her boys to difference, to disability, and to the world of color and diversity. There we met people in wheelchairs, drooling at the mouth, shaking with their limbs or whole body, people with no limbs but stumps, people who couldn't raise their hands to shake yours, people with big heads (hydrocephalics) or small heads (microcephalics), and people with deformities that either turned your head or tractor-beamed your eyes. This is where I learned the difference between the twisted spines of scoliosis and the hunchbacks of kyphosis. We met people there of every color and every shape. Mother taught us to look at every resident in the eye, to speak to them with respect, and never to show alarm or shock, regardless of what they looked like or what they did or didn't do. God loved each one of these people as much as God loved each one of us, and once we drank at the same fountain, we learned, differences didn't matter.

Our Sunday afternoon mission was to bring residents joy and sunshine for as long as we were there. When some "good church people" laughed at Mother for taking her boys to see such "gross" and "grotesque" people, Mother snapped back that the true "grotesques" were people who have allowed some idea or obsession to warp their lives and poison their souls.

Every trip to the county farm was preceded by a pep talk: Can you see eye to eye with these people? Not to agree, but to care? Not until you look into the eyes of neighbors and strangers, the ugly and the beautiful, at the table or on the porch, and listen to their stories, do they turn into human beings. To like only people like yourself is to worship yourself, which is to be captive and oppressor at the same time. When you are expected and pressured to think alike and talk alike and act alike and live alike, why is that not a new form of slavery?

I trace my lifelong obsession with gargoyles and misericords to these Sunday afternoons at the county farm. We were taught that people with disabilities and differences were not annoying diversions but anointed diversities. We were taught to enjoy people whom God made different and to never fawn over "the right people" as if we needed them in order to be "right" ourselves. It's okay to "butter your betters," Mother would say, even when you know better than your betters. But no one was "better than" anyone else—"and don't you forget it!" It is one thing to tolerate difference. It is another thing to celebrate all difference. But it is a Jesus thing to love one another in the throes of difference.

The literal meaning of *pagan* is "country dweller." The gospel was first proclaimed in Galilee—the place of Gentiles, the place of difference, the place where pagans or people from the "far country" dwelled. Jesus had no problem mixing and mingling with "pagans" and "sinners." The light is meant to shine in such far countries.

Mother staked her soul on there being one way to the Father—through Jesus Christ the Son—but she saw many ways to Jesus. You can say yes to your own tribe without saying no or "Get thee behind me, Satan!" to someone else's. Long before Richard Foster wrote *Streams of Living Water*,[1] Mother taught us that there were many ways to Jesus, but only the Jesus Way to God. There was the virtuous "holiness" tradition (her favorite), the Spirit-empowered "charismatic" tradition (our first cousin), the prayer-filled "contemplative" tradition, the compassionate "social justice" tradition, the Bible-centered "evangelical" tradition (epitomized by the Baptists), and the sacramental "incarnational" tradition (Lutherans and Anglicans). More than anything, this may explain why I am too mystical for the rationalists, too rationalist for the orthodox, too orthodox for the progressives, too progressive for the conservatives, too conservative for the academics, too academic for the charismatics, too charismatic for the Jesus-focused, and too Jesus-focused for everyone.

Mother did not believe that all religions were created equal. But she did believe we had something to learn from every religious tradition, and that exposure to other religions could make our faith stronger, not weaker. Although she would have rejected and resented the comparison, her position was not dissimilar to the official position of the Catholic Church toward other religions as elaborated in Vatican II, a development she tracked privately with great interest:

> The Catholic Church rejects nothing of what is true and holy in these religions. She regards with sincere reverence those ways of conduct and of life, those precepts and teachings. . . . The Church, therefore, exhorts [Christians] . . . [to] recognize, preserve and promote the good things, spiritual and moral, as well as the socio-cultural values found among these men.[2]

Duke Ellington grew up in the manse of his father's African Methodist Episcopal church. He always wore a gold crucifix around his neck and late in life began writing liturgical music and performing sacred concerts. His mother was an upscale Baptist, but she taught him that denominational tags didn't matter; only Jesus mattered. Sounds like he and I had the same mother—except mine was convinced that the holiness tradition offered the best reflection of Jesus' "mattering." Nevertheless, each tradition had something to offer the whole body of Christ that the others didn't, and we needed to learn from each as we all looked to Jesus. Quoting an old revival preacher, Mother said, "Jesus is coming back for a bride, not a harem."

In researching a book on Sunday schools, I ran across

the story of a little girl who was dusting the furniture in her grandmother's house. The grandmother, unsatisfied, said, "Dust it again." So the girl dusted it a second time, and a third, and a fourth. Finally she said, "Grandma, there's no dust on the furniture. The dust is on your glasses." In arranging for us to mix and mingle with difference, and especially with people who had physical and mental handicaps, we were constantly being forced to keep cleaner glasses through which to see others. Blind eyes are no disability in the long run. But blind minds are.

Someone once suffered a "nervous fit" at our local church one Sunday morning. Mother complained loudly about how the church handled it. "No room in church for a person with a need," she complained. She wrote in her notebook, "Room in church for more studies but not for needy souls."

When I first read some words of Thomas Aquinas (favorites of Pope Francis) in graduate school, they immediately brought to mind not a rainbow of colors but our friends at the county home: "His goodness could not be adequately represented by one creature alone. . . . For goodness, which in God is simple and uniform, in creatures is manifold and divided."[3] I have always felt a kinship with the Assemblies of God ever since a sign in front of one of their churches dropped the "G" to make it "Assemblies of od." God's odd is my kind of church. We are a peculiar people, afraid of our peculiarity. Calvary is a mount that can be glimpsed only from different sides. And the view from

Calvary is of outstretched arms that embrace the world. The Sweet Family was a guest of many Salvationist services, and Mother felt a special kinship with William and Catherine Booth, the Methodists who founded the Salvation Army. At a rally in London, William Booth famously shouted at the crowd, "How wide is the girth of the world?"

Back came the answer: "Twenty-five thousand miles."

To that Booth roared, "Then we must grow till our arms get right about it."

Mother encouraged us to be with people of different cultures, different races, and different nationalities. But she was most intentional with African Americans. We were Southerners, she said, but the part of the South that opposed slavery. She reminded us constantly that it was a black man who came to Jesus' aid and helped carry his cross. Mother loved sorghum, a product for "sweeting" food without sugar that made its way north before the Civil War as a way of avoiding complicity in the slave trade; she tried to get us to love it as well.

Although racial segregation was prevalent on Hungry Hill where we lived, Mother invited black friends to our house and—just as scandalous—went to black friends' homes. We ate at Melvina Norris's house with her family and played with whomever was there. On our birthdays, we got to invite one of Mother's friends to join us for the meal; my brother Phil chose Melvina (I got to choose Marion Lamb). We routinely prayed for Melvina at family prayer. "God deals with hearts, not races," she said when some of her friends criticized her friendship with Melvina. Mother even convinced Melvina to teach her Sunday school class when she was sick, which created quite a ruckus.

---

*Jesus is All. But our mission is to see that the All is "in all."*
MABEL BOGGS SWEET,
REFLECTION ON I CORINTHIANS 15:28

---

As a child, I may not have understood all of this immediately. But Mother's lessons seeped in and have become a firm part of my theology and my outlook on life. Yet I do have to say, the only thing better than having Jesus as your friend is having Jesus with a Mounds or Mars bar as your friend. Everyone knows, a young Lenny Sweet mused, that a Mars a day helps you and Jesus work, rest, and play better.

# 12

# THE MYSTERY BAG AND THE CURIOSITY CABINET

꩜

*In the Book of Acts the disciples sought out helpers. They
did not hunt for talents. They sought men and women
full of faith and the Holy Ghost. . . . When a miracle was
done, people honored God not the miracle-worker. The
disciples were channels. They did not channel themselves,
or their powers, only the Christ or the Holy Ghost.*

MABEL BOGGS SWEET

When Mother didn't "get" God about something, she
said we should "file that in the mystery bag." Then she
would often hum or sing the 1911 hymn "Farther Along":

*Farther along we'll know more about it,
Farther along we'll understand why;
Cheer up, my brother, live in the sunshine,
We'll understand it all by and by*

Some things you have to swallow whole, as an owl swallows a mouse, and let the stomach do the sorting out. And some things are not amenable to swallowing at all, in whole or in part; they are as dense and radioactive as plutonium. Some things are mysteries requiring resolution. You put them away in a root cellar, where the conditions are dry and cool, to keep them fresh.

When something went into Mother's "mystery bag," it was her way of refusing to make big bones about some very bare bones of understanding. Sometimes we don't have "realizations" so much as "wonderings" or "ponderings" or questions we can live with. Why do we have to always put things into words, instead of just leaving it with "taste and see that the LORD is good"?[1]

The deeper the faith, the greater the questions, the bigger the bag, and the grander the mystery of Thomas's resolution, "My Lord and my God!"[2] For Mother, the "mystery bag" was an offensive, not a defensive, weapon, as when Jesus asked the crowd one question that shut everyone up and shut everything down: "No one could say a word in reply, and from that day on no one dared to ask him any more questions."[3] Such is the power of the "mystery bag."

---

*It's good to ask questions. All questions are good. But people who are always asking questions aren't interested in answers but in causing confusion.*

MABEL BOGGS SWEET

---

*Mabel Boggs Sweet, 1912-1993*

## Minister's Annual Pocket Credential

DATE ____ 13, ____

THIS IS TO CERTIFY THAT:

_____ WAS, ON THE
DATE OF ISSUANCE HEREOF, AN ORDAINED MINISTER IN GOOD STANDING
IN THE PILGRIM HOLINESS CHURCH OF AMERICA.

_____ GEN. SEC'Y
VALID ONLY WHEN SIGNED BY THE GENERAL SECRETARY

_Robert L. Smith_ DIST. SEC'Y
AND COUNTERSIGNED BY THE DISTRICT SECRETARY

34 Highland Ave
Gloversville

_New York_                   _34 Highland Ave_
NAME OF DISTRICT          ADDRESS OF DIST. SEC'Y
THIS CREDENTIAL IS VALID FOR ONE YEAR FROM DATE OF ISSUE.

## Minister's Annual Pocket Credential

DATE _July 12, 1949_

THIS IS TO CERTIFY THAT:

_Mabel Sweet_ WAS, ON THE
DATE OF ISSUANCE HEREOF, AN ORDAINED MINISTER IN GOOD STANDING
IN THE PILGRIM HOLINESS CHURCH OF AMERICA.

_G.M. Stickelather_ GEN. SEC'Y
VALID ONLY WHEN SIGNED BY THE GENERAL SECRETARY

_Rev. Robert L. Smith_ DIST. SEC'Y
AND COUNTERSIGNED BY THE DISTRICT SECRETARY

_New York_                   _Gloversville, N.Y._
NAME OF DISTRICT          ADDRESS OF DIST. SEC'Y
THIS CREDENTIAL IS VALID FOR ONE YEAR FROM DATE OF ISSUE.

*Local preacher's license and credentials, renewed annually*

*The home on "Hungry Hill," 28 Bloomingdale Avenue, Gloversville, New York*

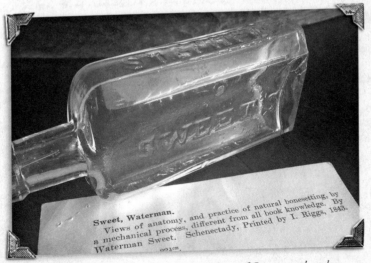

*Original bottle of Sweet's Liniment, with Library of Congress card catalog for Waterman Sweet's 1843 textbook on bonesetting*

*Graduating class of Allentown Bible School*

*Allentown Bible School ordained minister certificate*

# CAMP MEETING
## AT
# BLOXOM, VA.
# August 11-20

---

## Three Preaching Services Each Day

---

## *SPECIAL WORKERS*

Rev. G. A. Castevens, of Danville, Va.
**Evangelist**

Misses Mabel Boggs and Eunice Stone
Singers, Musicians and Young People's Workers

Rev. C. C. Elzey, of Bloxom, Va.

And Other District and Visiting Preachers

Rev. G. A. Castevens

Rev. C. C. Elzey

---

## Board and Lodging On the Grounds at Reasonable Rates

*Arrange to Spend These Ten Days With Us*

---

For further information, write Rev. C. C. Elzey, Bloxom, Va., or R. J. Rew, Onancock, Va.

*Camp meeting: the evangelical equivalent of a bat/bar mitzvah*

*The wedding of Mabel Boggs and Leonard Lucius Sweet. Mother was brought up on charges of worldliness for, among other things, bobbing her hair for her wedding, resulting in her being defrocked by the Pilgrim Holiness Church.*

MABEL V. BOGGS
Covington, Va.

ADVANCED THEOLOGICAL

"*Her vocation is to serve God and humanity.*"

*Pine Grove Camp-Meeting Quartet*

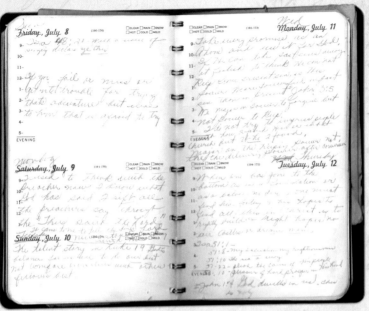

*Mother's yearly journals*

*A typical page in one of Mother's dozen study Bibles*

In tribute to

# Reverend Mabel Sweet

*A pioneer of women in ministry,*

*Who ministered in the Pilgrim Holiness Church,*

*And who stood by her convictions*

*At great personal cost.*

*Presented this 29th day of January 2015 by*

THE **wesleyan** CHURCH

Jo Anne Lyon, General Superintendent

*2015 recognition of Mabel Boggs Sweet by a denomination*
*that had defrocked her sixty years earlier*

Mother found the biblical warrant for the mystery bag in Revelation: "The temple was filled with smoke from the glory of God and from his power, and no one could enter the temple until the seven plagues of the seven angels were completed."[4]

No one can move when God speaks. No one can move when God changes the weather, changes the furniture, or changes the mission. "It is only Lord as you come upon me and move in me," Mother wrote, "that I can be or do, walk, or live, in a useful manner that brings glory to your name." Just because you don't understand something doesn't mean it's something to be scorned or smitten or something not worthy of standing under. Some things you are bagging because you don't understand them. Some things you are bagging because you can't explain what you know. As Augustine said, "If nobody asks, I know what it is; but when you ask me to explain, I can't do it."[5]

The statement that should send every theologian and teacher shaking in their boots? "[False teachers] blaspheme in matters they do not understand. They are like unreasoning animals, creatures of instinct, . . . and like animals they too will perish."[6] In other words, beware of speaking against (or for) things you do not understand or of condemning (or giving divine approval for) that which is beyond your current intellectual pay grade.

Some people try to turn faith into something mechanical, to make faith a mechanism for meaning. Mother was content to let faith remain a mystery. The essence of mystery, like the mystery of resurrection, is not that its meaning is inexpressible but that it is inexhaustible. I am a theologian of revelation that is (like resurrection) inexhaustibly intelligible. The moment you explain or exhaust the mysteries of faith to me is the moment I will cease to be a Christian.

A faith that "manifests the mystery" is not a passive faith, but the opposite. The word *manifest* in Greek is such a strong word; it means that you can physically detect it. Mother would often mutter, "Is it nothing to you, all you who pass by?"[7] under her breath when she saw Christians stand down when she thought they should stand up. How easy is it to pass by? Bypassers are bystanders to life—passengers when Jesus expects us to be drivers and conductors. To manifest the mystery was not to "pass it by" but to show passion and pass it on.

Besides being open to manifesting the mystery even more than brandishing the solutions, Mother encouraged us to take an interest in something without taking it in. She called this "curiosity," and believed that the church needed more-curious, not less-curious, Christians. Alongside her bag of mysteries stood a cabinet of curiosities.

---

*Don't preach what you comprehend of God. Preach God's Word as revealed by the Holy Spirit and leave the rest to God. God can level them out.*

MABEL BOGGS SWEET,

23 MAY 1957

---

"Curiosity cabinets" were creations of the Renaissance. Before museums became as we know them today, almost everyone of any means had one or two "museums" in their home called *kunstkabinetts* or *kunstkammers*—literally, "cabinets of art" or what we today call "curio cabinets." When you went to someone's home, one of the first things you visited was his or her curiosity cabinet. Sometimes a corner cupboard, sometimes a grand bookcase, sometimes a whole room, they were filled with a mishmash of objects, both natural and crafted, that showcased the wonders of the world and the character of the owner's imagination. In many ways these *wunderkammers* ("chambers of wonder") were the opposites of a museum: Unsystematic and idiosyncratic, they reflected a pre-Enlightenment amateurism. But they encouraged people to be curious about their world and to sip one of Alice's Wonderland potions occasionally when in need of a dose of the extraordinary.

Mother was constantly probing, in one fashion or another, what we were putting in our mystery bags and what we were featuring in our curiosity cabinets. We were taught that we were at our best when we were curious. This partly explains my love of antiques and of exploring those one-of-a-kind "Olde Curiosity Shoppes" that dot the blue highways of North America. Lack of curiosity and creativity are culture-killers. You can monitor a culture's curiosity levels by checking its patent registrations. Every successful person is creative, which means his or her life is becoming an "olde curiosity shoppe."

Tradescant the Elder was one of the most notable cabinet keepers in history. In 1625 he requested in a letter to the secretary of the English navy, "Anything that is strang [*sic*]."[8] The discovery of the strangeness of familiar-seeming things—in life and in the Scriptures—is what made Mother such a magnet. She had an uncanny knack for finding the strange and unfamiliar—in a text, in a context, or in a person. The unpardonable sin for any preacher in Mother's mind—besides not lifting up Christ—was to lift him up in a way that had a familiar feel, that repeated fashionable phrases and slogans, that told stories from a well-thumbed deck (a metaphor Mother would never have approved), that made Jesus so overfamiliar he became cozy and cosseted. She believed preachers ought to be on a campaign against cliché, whether of the mind, the heart, or the soul. (She was not averse, however, to using clichés to campaign against clichés.)

The opposite of cliché was strangeness, freshness, and energy. The more familiar the text, the more unfamiliar Mother's journey into the text. In making the Bible strange so it could become fresh again, Mother was instinctively doing what philosophers and rhetoricians have elaborated more formally. "*Was ist bekamt ist nicht erkannt,*" wrote German philosopher G. F. W. Hegel (1770–1831): "What is familiar is not known." The paradox that the closest things to you are the hardest things for you to see and perceive was common sense to Mother.

To make people uneasy with the familiar was the beginning of wisdom. But when people are shaken out of old habits and encouraged to see the world afresh, they often aren't grateful for the experience. If the "joy of the LORD" is the church's strength,[9] the jowls and scowls of the church are the Lord's manacling. I had a front-row seat to watch Mother wage ecclesiastical fights for her ministerial call and her spiritual joy. In this Mother had to deal with a double blowback. First, she had to deal with the fact that she was a woman preacher. As she reflected on Pilate's wife, "Nobody listened to a woman's dream then. And they aren't likely to listen to a woman's dream now."[10] English writer Virginia Woolf (1882–1941), who coined the term "life-writing," famously shared from personal experience that "as long as a woman talks of love, no one minds a woman talking." Unafraid of strong judgments, Mother reminded everyone who would listen that at a time when Jewish women were always in the background, Jesus brought them into the foreground of his stories and his everyday life. Mother took great comfort from the fact that women have come a long way from the days when even married women had no legal standing. In seventeenth-century England, husbands bequeathed to their wives their own clothes.[11]

Second, while Mother was a stirring stick that troubled the waters so healing could take place, the truth is that some people don't want to be healed. Moreover, some Christians have not just a chip on their shoulder, but the whole tree (and sometimes an entire forest). People are easier to criticize than to understand, but Jesus calls us not to criticism or cynicism but altruism. To be of service to God and others, there will be some sacrifice. The only chip on my mother's shoulder was the Cross, full of splinters, which she would always carry humbly and gladly. Sacrifice is the price of service.

Mother vented her frustrations over the criticisms she faced in three ways: She cried her heart out, she laughed her heart out, and she sang her heart out.

Jesus cried his heart out in Gethesmane. If Jesus had the need of doing that, Mother always felt she could too.

Mother thought you could substitute "laughter" for "love" in Paul's famous love chapter: "Laughter suffereth long, and is kind."[12] The devil never laughs, she insisted. That's why a sense of humor is required to ward off evil and temptation. A family of faith is a family of laughter. Little laughter? Little faith.

Finally, Mother sang. She turned her every activity into a sonic event. "They," she wrote in her notebook on 17 April 1979, referencing Matthew 26:30, "went out after singing a hymn. Only after a song were they able to face life."

This is how Mother kept her faith—a holistic faith comfortable with curiosity. Faith, she understood, is the eye that sees the Truth, the ear that hears the Song, the feet that walk the Way, the hands that touch the Unknown, the tongue that tells the Story, and the mind that stewards the Mystery.

# 13

# EXTRA PLATE AT THE TABLE

———— ❦ ————

*God is looking for full people to use . . . and empty people to fill.*
MABEL BOGGS SWEET

Life's greatest pleasures: coffee in the morning, getting lost in a book or song, sitting at table, the joy of friendship, worshiping God, and talking to you.

This is a good summary of mountain culture in general, and in particular Appalachian culture, a tapestry of subcultures that have been minimized as contributors to the wider USAmerican culture. Worse, Appalachian heritage has been dismissed by some cynics as nonexistent, except as the romantic creation of intellectuals.[1]

The concept of "homestead" or "homeland" is key to Appalachian culture. You may not live there, but you still have kin and kindred back in the mountains, and you return there for holidays, vacations, and ceremonies. A "stem family" has roots in Appalachia and branches in cities (especially of the Midwest). When you aren't in the homeland, you feel as if you are living in exile. For your cousins who stayed and didn't move away, you are an expatriate. You keep your "family ties" strong by listening to bluegrass music, eating down-home food, taking pride in your independence, and having your car packed and ready to "head for the hills" after work on Friday night. I've always liked Loretta Lynn's comment about Jimmy Carter's election: "I'm glad we finally have a President without an accent."[2]

As I have already intimated, I grew up in a cross-cultural home: a mother from the South, a father from the North. "Split at the root," as poet Adrienne Rich says of her own growing up.[3] What was common to both my parents was the part of the mountain where they were from: the bottom, where, in the words of Langston Hughes, "life . . . ain't been no crystal stair."[4]

The "home church" in our family homestead (Alvon, West Virginia, where my grandparents lived) was a Methodist church where, if Jesus didn't have a covered dish, they probably wouldn't let him in. All the churches in the holler were the same, except that the uppity Presbyterians called their potlucks "tureen suppers."

Appalachian hospitality is symbolized by the table, with the lazy Susan as its centerpiece. But unlike Asian cultures, where the lazy Susan is loaded with food, on the Appalachian revolving table you will often find, displayed for everyone to see, what most families hide in cabinets: favorite spices and condiments (especially vinegar) and medicines that members of the family are taking. When you are invited to an Appalachian home for a meal, the stories of that household are splayed out on that table before anyone says a word.

In Appalachian culture, the ultimate gift you can give someone is to go to their funeral—because you honestly can't expect anything from them in return. The second-highest gift you can give anyone is to invite them to your table. Appalachian culture is a lot like Semitic cultures, where if you share a cup of water with a stranger, you are friends for the day, and if you share a meal with a stranger, you become family. Relationships are built and strengthened by bread being broken and shared at the table.

In Hebrew culture, to welcome new members into the "family" was to "covenant" with them. The covenant Yahweh made with Israel meant that Israel was the "family" of Yahweh. A covenant involved three things: an oath, a sacrifice, and a shared meal. Jesus mentioned the "new covenant" only once, but it involved all three elements: an oath, a sacrifice (himself), and a shared meal.[5] The new covenant meal is the Eucharist. We partake of the table of the Lord.[6] Think about that for a moment: The Eucharist is, literally, the Lord's table. He is the host. We are his guests. Jesus did not host a seminar or a conference but a meal.

For me to tell you about the table I was at when I was a kid, and the stories I learned there, is for me to tell you the secrets of who I am. If we become the stories we tell, telling the right stories is how we overcome what we've become.

Leo Tolstoy famously wrote, "Happy families are all alike."[7] I disagree, except in one respect: All happy families keep the table sacred. The decline of Sunday lunch around the table and the rise of Sunday brunch around the TV has meant the loss of bonds between family and friends. We prefer to worship God in our way (on our way to lunch) rather than in God's way: "in the Spirit and in truth."[8] God's way of worship is at the table together.

Mother was not a cook and didn't pretend to be. She married late and had kids into her early forties, almost unheard-of at the time. Her mother, Ida, had married at sixteen; her older sister, Hattie, had married at age eighteen. Both were expert cooks, and Mother always deferred to them. She did resent her father, George Lemuel, for insisting that Ida get up every morning at 4 a.m. and make him biscuits. "I'm not getting up early to make biscuits for any man," she would say. She mocked the telegram she received after her wedding, congratulating her and offering this "Advice to the Bride":

*Meet him with a smile*
*Always go fifty-fifty*
*Make him hot-biscuits every morning*

In fact, I don't ever remember Mother making biscuits other than those in the tube that you hit on the counter, peel off from the pile, and put in the oven. When people ask what my mother's favorite dish was, I immediately default to Dad's cooking; his shopping and cooking kept us from starving.

But Mother did cook one meal a week: Sunday "dinner" (the meal after church). The menu was almost always the same: We would gather around fried chicken (the sacred bird) served with mashed potatoes and thick, pasty gravy made from the bottom of the skillet, some vegetables that came out of a can, and rolls (not biscuits). There was some form of Tropicana Salad (cottage cheese and canned fruit, usually mixed fruit or pineapple). My father usually made the dessert (his cherry cheesecake on graham cracker crust was my favorite). Sunday dinner was the biggest meal of the week, and every one was a symposium. In ancient Greece, the word *symposium* (literally "drinking together") meant a long night of food, conversation, and conviviality. Sunday dinner was all that; the drinking was always iced tea.

My brothers and I would set the table before we left for church. Mother would often set an extra plate, which she called "Elijah's seat." In most of Judaism, Passover includes an "Elijah's cup" filled with wine to express the hope that Elijah would be present to herald the coming of the Messiah. Some adult might furtively bump the cup of wine, spilling it so the kids would think Elijah had actually shown up. Since we didn't drink wine, Mother made it an empty seat, prepared in the spirit of the words spoken at Passover: "All those who are in need, come and eat!"

We knew what our empty seat meant: The Sweet family was expected to find some stranger or visitor to bring back with us for lunch. In my unsanctified moments, I thought, *Mother can't cook without making a show of it.* But in my more respectful moments, I realized that this was another form of evangelism that Mother was encouraging. If we failed to find someone to bring home for lunch, "Elijah's seat" would remain open as a silent rebuke to us for failing to show hospitality to strangers.

Over the years, our Elijah's seat was occupied by some strange table-mates. But at every table, Jesus was the host, and the Gospels the main fare. Why Jesus as host? Some things can fuel your mind and fill your belly but not feed your soul. Jesus at table does all three. Why Gospels as main dishes? Matthew gives us Jesus' pedigree, Mark gives us his destiny, Luke gives us his humanity, and John gives us his divinity. The Gospels are one four-faceted gem. (The top surface of a cut, faceted diamond is called a table.)

Our Sunday dinners included people with varying diets, appetites, and "-isms," but everyone left satisfied. In my early years Mother was very anti-Catholic. The Sweet family didn't even make the election of John F. Kennedy a matter of family prayer because Mother announced that in no way would God allow a Catholic to be elected president of a Christian nation. (When we awoke to news of his election, it was a clear sign to both my parents that the Rapture was not too distant.) Nevertheless, Catholics were welcome at our dinner table. One of the most unusual guests who ever sat in our Elijah's seat was a Russian Orthodox priest from Holy Trinity Monastery at Jordanville, New York, who became a close family friend and introduced the entire Sweet family to the world of Eastern Orthodoxy. We took a family trip to "the Jordan," where the seminary and monastery were located and where we met some other seminarians and were given Orthodox literature, which we took home and discussed.

Polycarp (69–155) tried to escape persecution, but when it became apparent that he was doomed, he prepared himself by cooking food for the soldiers who came to arrest him. Is there any better illustration of "You prepare a table before me in the presence of my enemies"?[9]

Jesus calls for the stranger as well as the enemy to have a place at the table. For those of us who have saved seats, it's time to move down, squish together a bit, invite some new faces, and put in some new leaves. If you find yourself always buying presents "for the person who has everything," maybe it's time to invite "the person who has nothing" to the table.

There is an old saying that parents owe children roots and wings. I learned from Elijah's seat to change that to roots and leaves. If the table is the tree of life, what do you do to enlarge a table? You add "leaves." The leaves are the "wings," and the legs of the table are roots that go down deep, deep into the soil, deep into the soul, of both a person and a community. What happens on the table strengthens the roots and sprouts new leaves.[10]

To love God is not the same thing as to love one's neighbor. To love God is to experience all of life through the lens and senses of Jesus, to frame all of life in a sacramental way, and to cultivate the art of reading the signs of Jesus' presence in the world. Loving God magnifies your range of awareness of the world, its ecstasies and agonies, its past and future, its wonders and wickedness. To love God is to make the world bigger.

To love one's neighbor is to love life itself. As a wise person once said, "If you love only your neighbor, you will not love your neighbor for long." To love one's neighbor means to love the neighborhood that surrounds your neighbor, the nature that makes the neighborhood possible, and the heritage and hopes that all of creation holds dear to its heart. In other words, to love one's neighbor turns the magnifier into a scope. To love one's neighbor is to make the world smaller.

Elijah's seat has opened me to new possibilities for the table in resolving disputes, finding common ground, and living up to the tabletop virtues Jesus taught us. Jewish scholar Peter Ochs is right: "There are resources *out* of this world for correcting the inadequacies *of* this world."[11] I am especially drawn to Ochs's scholarship, not just because he understands semiotics but because he has dedicated his life to reading Scriptures in the company of others. By "others" I mean bringing all of the Abrahamic traditions together at the same table to listen to each other "read" the same stories.

The ultimate reason for keeping Elijah's seat open at the Sweet house was so that we might be better evangelists for Jesus. It's a jungle out there, and as Mother said, "In the jungle, if you look like food, you will be eaten." Jesus calls us to look like food, the bread of life and cup of salvation, so people can taste and see that the Lord is good.

# 14

# DAD'S ROLLTOP DESK AND HIS SECRET COMPARTMENT

*Religion is weights. Faith is wings.*

MABEL BOGGS SWEET

From as early as I can remember, I coveted my father's middle name: "Lucius," the Latinate form of "Luke." My father had given me Ira as my middle name, in honor of his father.

Leonard Lucius Sweet (born 25 June 1914) started out as a bookkeeper at a local bank, then got promoted to teller in 1938, then to assistant cashier, a position he held until he was made "bank officer" just before retiring after thirty-eight years with the bank. He served with the Air Force from 1941 to 1945, and those military relationships became his community. The G. I. Bill of Rights, passed by Congress in 1944, was (according to my father) one of the greatest things that ever happened to this country. He was convinced that whatever the bill had cost would eventually be paid off by expanded tax revenues and the good will of grateful veterans. He expressed his own gratitude by becoming a member of every veterans group he could find: He was a Son of the American Revolution, commander of the American Legion Post, county treasurer of the American Legion, and treasurer of the Arthritis Fund, which helped a lot of veterans.

Before Dad met Mother, he was a theater buff. His greatest ambition in life was to write a historical play or to act. In 1932 he had a role in the play *Lena Rivers*. His all-time favorite program on the radio, which he listened to almost every evening during its short run in 1937–1938, was *Do You Want to Be an Actor?*[1] He kept a little blue book where he chronicled the shows he saw, and he affixed a review to each one. Dad would go to church on a Sunday morning, come home for "dinner," then go to a 1:30 movie. Dad saw so many shows (sometimes four a day) that he had trouble finding new ones to see. (He admitted in his blue book not just that he played blackjack, but that he went to "girl shows" on stage, whatever that meant.)

I knew Dad had a secret side to him, even if I didn't know what it was until long after he was gone. I once discovered a side door in his rolltop desk; behind that concealed door I found what I as a kid considered racy magazines: *Yank* (published by the Army), *Eyeful*, and other pulp and pinup magazines. Besides the fact that my brothers and I were alive, this secret compartment in his desk is the only evidence in my life that Dad ever discovered Victoria's secrets. (Every quarter Mother and Dad observed a sacramental Sunday afternoon "nap time"; they tried to enforce it, but I observed it mainly in the breach.)

Mother was quite shapely and received the "male gaze" frequently, but "God never called any woman to be a sex simble," as Mother spelled it. In 1928, when Mother turned sixteen, Granddad said he would buy a Whippet four-door Model A, with both a starter and a crank, if the salesman taught her how to drive. The Whippet salesman tried to teach her more than that, making passes at her. She didn't tell her father because, in her words, "He would have killed him." This was not a metaphor, and Granddad had trouble keeping men from Mother until she moved away from home.

As children my brothers and I weren't permitted to go to the movies because Mother believed cinema was mind molestation: Seeing images of violence or rebellion could cause juvenile delinquency—or worse, parental defiance. But I learned in Mother's critique of movies that an ethic of images was as morally significant as an ethic of words. Just as there are certain words you should never say (and if you do, there are cleansing rituals to purify the mouth and mind), so there are certain images you should never see. Images have the power to shape reality, so much so that movies invariably end up first on the list of things that influence our destiny (followed by TV, Internet, books, public officials, and parents).[2]

Don't believe me? You kiss the way you do because of motion pictures. Movies fetishized kisses, which were never so prolonged (or wet) in previous centuries as they have been since *The Kiss* (1896), one of the first films ever shown. (The film is just eighteen seconds long, making it a short kiss by today's standards.) Or ask the Mafia, which has been as much created by as it was an inspirer of the movies. The New York Mafia was basically washed up in the early 1970s when *The Godfather* came out and told them who they were—not thugs but a new generation of immigrants out to get their piece of the American pie and to make the dream of the Promised Land come true. Thus began their comeback. The mafiosi got new life as they attempted to look and act like their screen images.

The pouring power of movies was brought home to me in the first movie I ever saw. I can still remember the naughty excitement of sneaking out of the house after screwing up my courage by listening to the Beach Boys song "Good Vibrations." I had no idea what was playing at the theater, and I found myself at the premier showing of Michelangelo Antonioni's *Blow-Up* (1966). In that film, a photographer accidentally captures with his camera what appears to be a murder in a London park. But when he tries to enlarge the shots, the images get cloudy and blurred. The photographer learns that we see what we want to see, or what we are trained to see, or what we believe we see—a message reinforced by an unforgettable tennis match played without a ball.

I shall never forget that film's impact on me, tipping, tilting, tempting. Pablo Picasso was talking of all art when he said, "Art is a lie that makes us realize truth,"[3] but the ability of *Blow-Up* to defamiliarize the familiar—to make me see that looking itself is subjective and partial and contextual—is a lesson I've never forgotten. The need for life to be constantly tilting, pouring, and in motion, and the inability of still photography to capture truth, has stayed with me, even in the form of a prejudice against still-life paintings.

I found myself so heated up about the movie that I couldn't stop talking about it. I encouraged all my friends to go see it, so we could compare notes and talk about it together. Unwittingly, I had become an evangelist, and to this day I use enthusiasm for a good movie to illustrate the difference between an evangelism of *invitation* and an evangelism of *imposition*. To share your excitement over a movie or book you've enjoyed is not to impose your judgments on anyone but to invite them to share your joy with you.

I sensed from Mother the notion that God is better than sex. (With that sensibility came the suspicion that there is something deeply sensual about union and communion with the divine.) Even the birds-and-bees conversation that Dad had with me when I turned thirteen eroded eroticism instead of exciting or explaining it. Perhaps that was the idea.

Told one Sunday evening that I was not going to church but was staying home with Dad, I wondered what was going on. I needed to go to church that evening as a member of the "Sword Drill" team. Once my brothers and mother had left, Dad sat me down across from him in the living room. Without looking me in the eye, he said: "You know the principle of the bolt and the screw?"

"Yes, sir," I replied. "I do."

"Good, then you know what you need to know about sex. Let me tell you about venereal disease."

For the next hour he regaled me with stories of STDs that he had learned about from Army and Air Force films. That was also the first time I understood why "screw you" was a swear word.

Mother never papered over the ways in which people in the Bible could be close to God and far from the ways of holiness. But the sexual components of these stories were never addressed. Longitudinal studies show that sexual addiction follows in the trail of two incubators: (1) violent, abusive families; or (2) rigid, repressive religious families. I've never been convinced of that second connection, but I do know from my own story of the failure of the evangelical tradition in particular and Christianity in general to embrace a healthy and whole human sexuality.

For me that larger failure is shown in paradigmatic fashion at the 1553 trial of Michael Servetus (1509–1553) in John Calvin's Geneva, which resulted in his being burned at the stake as a heretic. Among all the other theological charges, the Spanish theologian and physician Servetus was attacked for not having a wife and for showing symptoms of a sexually transmitted disease called *scortatim ac adulterio* (allegedly caused by having sex with prostitutes or committing adultery). Servetus strenuously denied the charges, and in his defense admitted that he had not married because of sexual inadequacies resulting from a botched operation when he was five, most likely an unsuccessful castration done with the intention of entering him into the papal choir.[4]

Holiness theology, or "the doctrine of Christian perfection," is often caricatured as the claim to live a "sinless life." To be sure, some of Wesley's descendants did huff and puff the bluff and bluster of perfectionism. When I was just a kid and barraged by the legalism of "don'ts," I came to the conclusion that if there was something I liked to do, I would someday, sooner or later, hear a sermon by some holiness preacher attacking it.

Mother herself could huff and puff "holier-than-thou" when she professed a "pure heart," which meant that whatever flowed from that intention, whether it be a fault or a failure, could not be a "sin" because "my heart is pure," she said. Nothing drove me from Mother more than this "righteous cover," which is what she called it when she found it in others. Mother coupled what scholars call Wesley's "optimism of grace" with a "pessimism of sin," but it still led her to refuse to recite general confessions of sin as liturgy, to refuse to sing the third verse of "Come Thou Fount" because of that phrase "Prone to wander, Lord, I feel it."

There is hokum, and there is holy hokum. But in

either case, it's still hokum. Even Paul didn't excuse himself because his will was pure; he admitted that he "willed" to do good but still did evil.[5] Lucretius' horrific line, *Tantum religion potuit suadere maloram* ("The greatest evil is done by religion"), stands as a perpetual rebuke to the doctrine of "good intentions." I didn't like the "righteous cover" in Mother, and I didn't like it when I found it in the Kantian dictum "There is nothing anywhere in the world, . . . even outside it, that could be considered good without limitation, except only a *good Will*."[6]

It took a long journey into theology for me to understand the word *holiness*. The word *holocaust*, which originally described a sacrifice totally consumed on the altar, once represented the ultimate in holiness: a sacrifice where nothing is saved, where all is laid on the altar. The fall of this word began with the words "They took the money and did as they were told."[7] This phrase, "they did as they were told," is the refrain of every holocaust of horror. The refrain of every holocaust of holiness, by contrast, is "They did what God said."

The best of holiness theology is to see salvation as a three-dimensional spiral, where the synergy of justification, sanctification, and glorification is always at play, and where sanctification really means, "It does not yet appear what we shall be."[8] Encounter Jesus, and you'll discover you've been talking gibberish all your life. Justification is when you start talking prose. Sanctification is when you start talking poetry. (Glorification is when you start singing.)

Sanctification is the process of cutting a raw diamond in order to create a gem diamond. Only the most skilled artisan can bring out the beauty of a raw diamond, and the Holy Spirit is the master gem cutter.

When Mother referred to Jesus as "the Way," she meant the "straight and narrow" way. But the older Mother got, the more she discovered that there's a wideness in God's mercy. For me this was the proof of Mother's sanctification: She became less legalistic and more libertarian the older she became. With every passing year she seemed to become more mellow, less focused on the "don'ts" and more on the "dos." She found new meaning in the "soul liberty" of the Baptists, or what Paul called "the glorious liberty of the children of God":[9] "If the Son sets you free, you will be free indeed."[10] She sipped her first beer in her sixties, at my brother Phil's wedding in Germany.[11] She no longer harangued me when I offered guests wine at my dining room table when she lived with me during my presidency of United Theological Seminary. (Since I was single at the time, she functioned as the First Lady of the President's house and hosted many functions for me, including one with Willie Nelson and Nancy Wilson.) She even started dating a distinguished gentleman from across the street, David Allman.

Freedom in Christ liberates us for a more open, creative, artistic attitude toward life: a nonidolatrous embrace of artefacts that art our life story[12] and a life that extends relationships and embraces community.

*Moses' Mother feared not kings' command and hid Moses. Moses feared
not kings' wrath and led the Israelites from out of bondage to Egyptians.
But only God through Jesus can give us total deliverance or freedom.*

MABEL BOGGS SWEET,

21 JANUARY 1957

Once at United Theological Seminary, my Sunday morning schedule opened up to where I could take Mother to
church. She usually worshiped at one of the three United
Methodist churches in northwest Dayton, Ohio, but many
of her friends attended Fairview, so that's where we went. The
first people we met walking up the stairs were friends from
her Free Methodist past who were visiting the church themselves. When I first saw them I thought I had stepped into a
time warp from my past: He was wearing a frumpy, crumpled
dark suit; she wore an ankle-length dress "without adorn-
ment" (no jewelry), and her long hair was in that signature
bun. I vaguely remembered this couple being mentored by
Mother at our home on Hungry Hill. The first thing Mother
did, of course, was invite them to join us for Sunday dinner,
which they gratefully accepted.

After the service, Mother gave them directions to our
Ravenwood Avenue house in Upper Dayton View. She
instructed them to wait for us in the driveway, since she
needed to stop at the store for some lettuce. I drove to the
closest supermarket I could find, ran in to get the lettuce

she needed, and rushed back to the house, where they were waiting for us at the back door. We had a wonderful time of conversation about the "good ol' days" as Mother set a couple of Elijah seats at the table.

When we all sat down, I asked if one of them would like to grace the table. The husband shyly agreed but prayed quite nervously. I wondered what was wrong, but dismissed my reading as not really knowing these people. Both of them took portions of everything but politely declined to take salad. I was surprised when Mother aggressively passed the salad around again; again they refused. I could tell Mother was getting angry, but I had no idea why. For the third time, Mother passed the salad around the table, which once again was politely refused.

Then it happened. Mother stood up and said, "I know why you're not eating my salad. It's because I bought the lettuce on the Sabbath, isn't it? You mean to tell me that your soul is still laboring under that legalism? Don't you know that for freedom Christ has set you free? You need to be set free today!" And she began her sermon right there at the table about how more people are living behind bars than are actually behind bars and how freedom is less about physical location than Jesus-location.

I got up from my seat at the other end of the table, walked over to Mother, put my arm around her, calmed her down, and apologized as best I could to our guests.

It was the proudest I've been of Mother in my life.

# 15

# GRAMMA'S GREEN
# PORCELAIN WOOD STOVE

❦

*The issue is not "How big is your world?"*
*but "How big is your heart?"*
MABEL BOGGS SWEET

In Appalachian culture, feuds that simmer for centuries can be ignited by who has which of the family jewels. Mountain "family jewels" aren't gemstones or valuables but those things most dense with memories and narratives—like my Granddad's double-barrel, twin-gauge shotgun (cousin Timmy got it, the stinker); or my Gramma's porch swing (cousin George B. got that after I schemed for years); the English-German family Bible (in cousin George C.'s possession); or even the homestead outhouse (which was destroyed because no one wanted a "Yankee" to have it).

*The people only saw Jesus as a prophet and a native of Galilee. How sad to be so near and yet so far. We are as near to God or as far from God as our hearts.*

MABEL BOGGS SWEET,
REFLECTING ON MATTHEW 21:3-11

But the two most sought-after Boggs family jewels were Gramma's stove and Granddad's kettle. My cousin George and his wife, Jean, spent years traveling all over Virginia and West Virginia looking in antique stores for Gramma's green porcelain wood stove. (Mother joked that we had put Gramma Boggs on a pedestal: "We had to do something to keep her away from Granddad.") Up until her dying day, Gramma insisted on cooking on this stove. Every one of her children, as well as most of her grandchildren, offered to buy her a new stove. She could choose whether it was electric or gas. It made no sense. Why would she do this to herself? Mother argued with her over and over again: Everything would be so much easier on a modern stove. You wouldn't need someone to bring bins of wood into the house. You wouldn't need someone to cut logs into sizes that would fit into the stove. You wouldn't need someone to buy matches, and then someone to help get the fire started so the wood could start cooking (that's where she used me the most).

But Gramma would have none of it. She had raised fourteen children (only nine of whom lived) on this stove. And she would never cook on anything else.

Eventually it hit me: For Gramma, cooking was not just about food; cooking was about relationships. Gramma wasn't into efficiency and speed and independence. For her the stove was the conduit and conductor of relationships with her children and grandchildren.

Relationship is life; lack of relationship is death. Relationship is heaven; lack of relationship is hell. The good we do is for relationship.

God made planet Earth round: a globe, a sphere. This guarantees that we end up bumping into one another. The more you travel in the opposite direction from someone, the more likely you are to run into them. Sooner or later, hard as we try otherwise, we run into one another. How will we face off? Will we "square off" or encircle?

There is an old story about a merchant who left his house every day. His little boy remained at home. One day pirates and thieves came and robbed the house and burned it. When the merchant came back he saw the charred body of a child and believed it was his son who had died. He cried and beat his chest. He tore out his hair. He reproached himself for having left his child at home. And then he performed the funeral rites. He cremated the body of that child and carried the bag of ashes with him wherever he went. When he ate, he had the bag. When he worked, when he slept, always he had the bag with him.

As it turns out, the child had been kidnapped by the

pirates. A few months later, he was released. He returned home and knocked on the door. "Father," he said, "I'm back." But the father did not believe it. He believed his child had already died. So he refused to open the door. And the child finally had to go away.[1]

We can be so committed to "beliefs" and "propositions" and "truths" and "dogma" that when the real truth comes, the truth we've always been looking for and lovingly waiting for, we can't recognize it. Or to put it another way: How many parents have sacrificed relationships with their children for the sake of their principles?

Principles become pedestal statues and marble plinths that we put on the shelf and admire from a distance. Love doesn't want to be left on the shelf. Love wants no distance. Love wants to be picked up, to become a part of us. Love wants incarnation.

My mother had a best friend named Mary Elizabeth ("Sis Bet") Bray (1914–1998). They met at Allentown Bible Institute and stayed friends for over sixty years, during good times and difficult times (hospitalizations, surgeries, mental breakdowns, financial traumas, and betrayals of family and friends). They kept in touch until the very end by mailing each other messages in their own language that special friends sometimes create—in their case, Bible shorthand. Every letter was written in the same code but with different coordinates. For example, this is from the last letter Mother received from Sis Bet, two weeks before Sis Bet died: "I am in Deuteronomy and your name appeared

30:20, 31:6 & 8." That was how these best friends talked. They read the Bible with each other in mind and then kept track of passages that had the other person's "name on it."

These letters were always the same—simple, short, but packing a profoundly personal punch. I looked up the passages with Mother's "name on them"—the last words Mother heard from her best friend:

> That you may love the LORD your God, that you may obey His voice, and that you may cling to Him, for He *is* your life and the length of your days; and that you may dwell in the land which the LORD swore to your fathers, to Abraham, Isaac, and Jacob, to give them.[2]

> Be determined and confident. Do not be afraid of them. Your God, the LORD himself, will be with you. He will not fail you or abandon you.[3]

> GOD is striding ahead of you. He's right there with you. He won't let you down; he won't leave you. Don't be intimidated. Don't worry.[4]

Sis Bet was a Pilgrim Holiness/Wesleyan all her life; when I roomed with her for a semester of college, part of my "room and board" was to be music director at her church, Asbury Wesleyan, in Richmond, Virginia. But down deep Sis Bet believed that the Mennonites were closer to heaven than anyone else, and she dressed and acted accordingly. She would be "Holy Ghost happy" to know that I sent my youngest son, Egil, to a Mennonite Brethren School (Tabor College in Hillsboro, Kansas) and that I teach there part-time myself.

I had the privilege of caring for Mother during the last eleven years of her life. When the mother of Denise Levertov died after a lengthy illness that left her incontinent, with tubes in her nose and sores all over her body, the poet wrote a poem about her "laggard death," wishing for something quite different for herself:

> *O Lord of mysteries, how beautiful is sudden death*
> *when the spirit vanishes*
> *boldly and without casting*
> *a single shadowy feather of hesitation*
> *onto the felled body.*[5]

A woman named Betsy Barron describes caring for her own mother during the last illness of her life like this:

There is a strange heightening of life that takes place if we live within the sight of the end of life. There is acute sadness, but also a deep beauty to each moment. It is like standing with a foot in two kinds of streams. One stream is made up of grocery shopping and paying the bills and rotating the tires. The other stream is made up of tenderness and hope and love beyond imagining, of the widest and deepest stretches of the human spirit.

To live like that, aware of these two streams . . . is to hold up the finiteness of human existence against the infinite burning glass of God's eternal love.[6]

I felt these two streams come together during the last time Mother saw Sis Bet in person. Calling it her "last trip," Sis Bet came to Dayton to visit Mother. I took them to a holiness camp meeting at God's Bible School in Cincinnati. During the singing of the hymns, I saw these two friends sneak a look at each other and smile with the gleam of heaven in their eyes.

# 16

# THE DOCTOR'S SCRIPT

*Lenny said he was going to "live it up after exams." I am sure he did not mean it as it sounded, but may he never live it up today so it will take all tomorrow to live it down.*

MABEL BOGGS SWEET

My brothers and I attended the public school system. But when it came to Christianity, we were schooled at home. Homeschooling is not an option for a Christian, my mother believed. She cited Susanna and John Wesley to back her up. I was never sure whether Mother was just making some of this stuff up, but later I read church historian Gayle Carlton Felton (1942–2014) make Mother's case: "Wesley realized that the home influenced the lives of children even before the church, and that parents were, for good or evil, the first religious teachers of their children."[1]

Mother turned her child-rearing principle into a

motto—"Children need to be insulated, not isolated"—
and a mantra: "Insulate, don't isolate." Children, Mother
believed, should be so prepared and protected by the
armor of truth that they grow stronger from resisting the
enemy. My brother John, whose doctoral dissertation at
the University of Berlin was on John Milton, reminded
me that Milton's *Areopagitica*, as part of its defense of the
freedom of the press, talked about "the true wayfaring
Christian" in these terms:

> I cannot praise a fugitive and cloistered virtue,
> unexercised and unbreathed, that never sallies out
> and sees her adversary but slinks out of the race,
> where that immortal garland is to be run for, not
> without dust and heat. . . . That which purifies us
> is trial, and trial is by what is contrary.[2]

Once we are baptized, we are united to Christ. We become something different, new creatures in Christ. We
are now the sons and daughters of God; we have put on
Christ; the Kingdom of God is within us; we have God's
Spirit in us; Christ lives in us; and we have put on the new
human.[3] In 1 Peter 1:4 the Greek word translated "inheritance" (*kleronomia*) refers to possessions passed down from
generation to generation, like the artefacts of this book.
You receive them as gifts, not because you earned them
or purchased them but because you're a member of the
family. By Christ being born in us, we receive our eternal

inheritance as children of God's family and citizens of the Kingdom of Christ.

---

*Some bear his name but not . . . his image.*
MABEL BOGGS SWEET

---

But to be united to Christ means you can't be untied from the world around you. And the options are more than either *detente* (liberalism) or *cordon sanitaire* (Anabaptism or holiness Wesleyanism). To be "in but not of" the world means the church approaches the world at a slight angle to the culture. This slant is not fearful of the world, and it even learns from the world. Sometimes the slant is tilted more in the direction of an alternative reading of reality than toward God's grace at work in the troublesome realities of the world. But there is a sense that if the church is to be in but not of the culture, there will be some things from the culture in our churches—such as pianos (an instrument that, along with the television, got Mother in such hot water with Dad's Free Methodist tribe).

In the middle of the second century, Justin Martyr taught that the *Logos* was at work not only in those who called themselves Christians but in all humanity. It's a line of thought that can be traced from Clement of Alexandria and Justin Martyr to Bonaventure to Luther to Wesley and Mabel Boggs Sweet. Mother never had trouble with Jesus telling his first disciples that we can learn from "the people of this world."[4] In fact, I have Mother to thank for my getting criticized all the time for quoting people who are not "believers." I even got called on the carpet during a nationally syndicated radio interview for quoting Jesus and Miss Piggy on the same page of one of my books.[5]

Mother was right. Everyone has something to teach you. Even Miss Piggy and the rest of pop culture. Augustine and Thomas Aquinas took the best thinkers of their time and used them to introduce Christ to their culture. Aquinas responded to critics of this practice by saying, "Do not heed by whom a thing is said, but rather what is said you should commit to memory."[6]

The slant meant to be "on time" in every culture but only "in time" with God's Spirit. "God's clock keeps perfect time" was one of Mother's favorite phrases. Satan always shows up "on time." But Satan never keeps God's time or stays "in time" with truth and beauty and goodness.

But the slant does not let the world have the last word. "Only The Word has the last word," Mother insisted. This is where the Boomer church has gone so wrong. Artificial injections of corporate strategies, programs, and skills produce a Botox bride—a body of Christ puffed up in toxic beauty and wearing the war paint of the world.

Mother took the slant one step further. We were strongly (and wrongly) encouraged not to "love the world or anything in the world,"[7] a verse which needed but seldom got its counterpart, "For God so loved the world."[8] Jesus didn't come to save souls but to save "the world"—and everything in it.

My brothers and I figure that Mother spent at least four hours a day teaching us in one form or another. All our public schooling was paralleled with a homeschooling that often conflicted with and protested the public schooling. Seldom did these fights over the slant involve the teachers and administrators themselves. But there were two exceptions.

Mother fought publicly with the school administration over the teaching of my sixth-grade teacher, Miss Catherine Hoffman, on evolution. Mother's conflict wasn't so much over evolution as science as it was over evolution as a new religion or a new battering ram against religion. As Francis Collins knows above everyone else, it isn't easy to defend evolution when faith's enemies use it against faith.

Long before Richard Dawkins and other atheists made Darwin and evolution the enemy of religion, Mother was battling this fight in the Park Terrace Elementary School in Gloversville, New York. Mother even suspected Darwin was right about some things. Her holiness bent opened her to a developmental understanding of Christianity, and there wasn't a big shift from God creating all things to God creating all things to create things. In fact, Charles Darwin himself was a theistic evolutionist who went to Cambridge to be a clergyman. He didn't abandon Christianity until midlife.

Yet Darwinist determinism smacked too much of Calvinist determinism for a die-hard Wesleyan like Mabel

Boggs Sweet. Evolution is a biological theory. We have made it into a worldview and faith system. The human mind needs to be shaped by the mind of Christ, not by the mind of science. Charles Darwin won the world over not by sheer science but by the brilliant metaphors he used to communicate his findings. Mother didn't have the theoretical tools or semiotics to express it this way, but she sensed a bigger game at play in the evolutionary debate. Evolutionary theory was not just freighted with metaphor but formed by it, and those metaphors were, she believed, nightmarish ones for the future.

The second arena where Mother fought the public school system was in the matter of dancing. Dancing was against our religion. Period. One of the most humiliating moments of my adolescence was when Mother discovered that a dance was the special event of a junior-high youth meeting. Unfortunately, she discovered this in the middle of the meeting—which didn't stop her from getting into the car, driving to the church, and storming into the church basement. She saw me struggling to dance, marched into the middle of the dance floor, grabbed me by the ear, and marched me out of the church. The pastor, Walter J. Whitney, followed us out and tried to plead my case with Mother. It didn't help when he said, "If Lenny did that well when he never danced before, all the more power to him." She always held those words against him.

Mother protested the mandatory dancing of our gym class in the public school. The administration insisted that dancing was a form of exercise, and that it was part of the required curriculum. When Mother refused to back down and was told "religious reasons" weren't sufficient to get us out of the state requirement, Mother declared it time to move into "wise-as-serpent-innocent-as-dove" mode.[9] She dressed us up and carted us all to our family physician. She informed the dazed doctor that he was to write each of us a "medical excuse" that would exempt us from dancing in school.

Our physician protested that he had never heard of such a thing. Besides, we were all fit to take gym and to dance. But Mother could dominate a room simply by being in it if she wanted to, and this was one time she wanted to. She countered that we were followers of Jesus, and Jesus didn't dance, so we weren't going to dance either. As we were his patients, he had the responsibility to get us out of dancing.

He dutifully got out his prescription pad and, in long-hand script, wrote out a "medical excuse" for Lenny, Phil, and John that prescribed absences from dancing "for religious reasons." He kept his medical integrity, while we got his medical cover. It was my first education in the power of white coats over black bathrobes: Doctors, not pastors, were exempting "the Sweet boys" from school activities "for religious reasons."

My whole ministry is both a reaction against my upbringing and a reflection of it. While I couldn't understand Mother's ways of thinking in terms of theology, to this day I have Baptist feet and can't dance. Nor have I ever understood "happy hour." Yet as a scholar and theologian,

I live and write the slant. Your stance in the circumstance makes all the difference in life—indeed, it is the very substance of life. In my scholarship I strive to slant the Jesus absolutes of love and faith and hope within the relative realms of cultures and contexts, to bring the Jesus absolute to life in the relative realms of every postal code.

# 17

# NAUTICAL DOOR

*When we pray for only that which we comprehend
or figure out it's not faith, and it's not prayer.*

MABEL BOGGS SWEET

Augustine (354–430) said that his mother lived on prayer. So did mine. She wore with pride the badge of a "praying mother" and believed that God could not resist the petitions of a mother at prayer.[1] As she put it, "Praying hands can bridge any gap and reach from earth to heaven."

Mother faced every new day the way Mary Magdalene faced resurrection morning. Mary, whose feast day (22 July) now has the same liturgical status as the twelve apostles', stayed awake and met the dawn while Peter and John returned home and went to bed. As such, she was the first to enjoy a Christophany—the first witness to Jesus, giving her the official title "apostle to the apostles" because she prayed through her pain and confusion and greeted the new day in a posture of prayer.

Mabel Boggs Sweet made prayer her first priority of the day, and she arranged the rest of her life accordingly. When the going got tough, Mother would send us to our room, quoting Jesus, who told his followers, "Go to your room."[2] For Jesus this was not a "time-out" but a time-in—making room in one's life for prayer, shutting the door on outside distractions, taking problems to God, and paying attention less to the problem than to what God is doing. When Jesus said, "Go to your room," he meant, "Look unto me and live."

Any room could become a "prayer closet," from a closet to a cathedral. Sometimes Mother would playfully throw an apron over her head, invoking the example of Susanna Wesley, who taught her children to leave her alone to pray whenever they saw her with her apron over her head. That was her place of prayer. John Wesley himself testified to the power of a praying mother.

Mother's favorite "prayer closet," however, was a "prayer meeting." A good prayer meeting was Mother's idea of a good party, for then the Spirit was her dance partner. There was so much prayer going on in our house it almost seemed an act of supererogation, even superficiality, to say a prayer before meals. Even Mother's mandatory prayer plant was ubiquitous, as every room seemed to need its own prayer plant.

*Your faith should not stand on the wisdom*
*of man but on the power of God.*

MABEL BOGGS SWEET

Mother's prayers were nothing more nor less than her conversations with Jesus. She prayed for people (especially her boys), and she asked for things. She loved to quote Psalm 37:4 (KJV)—"Delight thyself also in the LORD: and he shall give thee the desires of thine heart"—which meant that petitionary prayer was no harder for her than intercessory prayer. If our delight is in the Lord, then our desires are purified, and God delights to give them to us.

Too often we allow our worship and prayers to become beautiful bouquets masking excuses.[3] Of the thousands of prayers I heard Mother utter over the course of her lifetime, not once did I sense either a bouquet of words accompanying weak exercises of faith, or the perfume of an empty vase. When Mother prayed, it was as if she was releasing the most powerful force in the universe.

Mother died of congestive heart failure, which basically means she suffocated to death. As I sat by helplessly during her last days of gasping and gulping for air, she asked me to read out loud some of her favorite biblical passages. She'd throw out some passages, and I'd read her requests. Sometimes she'd forget what she had asked, so I'd read her the same passage over and over. Psalm 51:10 was one of those: "Create in me a clean heart, O God; and renew a right spirit in me" (KJV). It was as if she couldn't get enough of that verse. I can't remember for sure, but it may have been the verse that ushered her into eternity.

After Mother died, my spirit went into a tailspin. I didn't worry about it at first, since I knew souls have seasons—not linear seasons, like autumn following summer, but spiral seasons, where winter can follow spring and autumn can follow winter. (Artists go through seasons or phases; it took Picasso a while to get out of his "Blue Period.") Since work has always been my antidepressant, and my only real innate gift and talent is for incessant work, I just worked harder and ignored my disquiet.

But when people started noticing that something was wrong—"Sweet, you seem troubled! You okay?"—I decided that maybe this was that looming "midlife crisis" that Dante first warned us about: "Midway upon the journey of our life I found myself within a forest dark, / For the straight-forward pathway had been lost."[4] Or maybe it was something deeper going on. After all, Jesus came to bring peace and to be our peace, but he also came to disturb the peace and to be our disturber.

That was when I began praying in earnest for the Spirit to heal my spirit: to put in me the same "right spirit" that David had been praying for in Psalm 51, his great song of repentance—my reading that Mother turned into reverie. That's when the Spirit spoke to me, softly at first, then more insistently as time went on: "Read the psalm." I resisted because I knew the psalm. "Create in me a clean heart, O God; and renew a right spirit in me." I kept reciting it over and over again to myself as I had done to Mother. But the Spirit kept saying, "Read the psalm." Finally, after months of this annoyance in my head, it hit me that this verse that had been sustaining me was like a plaster cast that sustains a broken limb. For true and total healing to take place, it had to be removed. I had to remove myself from the verse and exercise movement in the whole psalm.

So I reread the entire psalm, not just verse 10, and discovered in the psalm the "right spirit" that drew strays and outcasts to Mother like a magnet, that describes in shorthand the essence of a "Jesus spirit," and that set my soul in motion once again.

After verse 10, David outlines two characteristic features of a "right spirit" that God will restore to his soul. And those two features are the harmonization of opposites: confidence and humility.

We all dwell in castles of deceit and delusion. Our biggest human malfunction and collective delusion is this: "I am, and there is none besides me."[5] Humanity without humility is the very definition of inhumanity.

But confidence is not arrogance when it's yoked to humility. I read once that the Romans and Greeks did not have a word for humility; they despised the attitude that it fostered. Judaism first made humility a virtue, as it was humility of spirit that ensured God's abiding presence and harbingered the only human hope of greatness.[6]

*Humility* is similar to the word *glory* in that it is frequently used in Scripture, is absolutely essential in our walk with God and with others, and is highly misunderstood. When the Bible says we are to "do nothing out of selfish ambition," it is not lambasting the desire to be excellent at something.[7] There was all too much groveling in the dirt, Mother felt, and when we started groveling, for whatever reason, she'd mock us: "Everybody hates me, nobody loves me, I guess I go to the garden and eat worms."

Humans are God's highest creation, not "imbecile worms of the earth," as Pascal called us. In fairness to Pascal, however, consider the stereophonic, humble-confidence context of the whole quote: "What a chimera then is man! What a novelty! What a monster, what a chaos, what a contradiction, what a prodigy! Judge of all things, imbecile worm of the earth; depositary of truth, a sink of uncertainty and error; the pride and refuse of the universe!"[8]

The danger is "selfish ambition," which is the desire to be better than others so that you will have more—more visibility, notoriety, appreciation. This is when you get, from Mother's quiver of metaphors, "too big for your britches," "high and mighty," "too high on the horse," or "a head too big for the body." Her worst condemnation of a preacher was to say, after which nothing more need be said, "They've lost the common touch." Or as Mother put it in more original form, "We all think we're special. Thinking you're special is what it means to be just like everyone else. The really special people are those who know Jesus is special and let Jesus 'special' them."

To turn this teaching of Mother into iconic form, I have installed a nautical door to my study. To enter my study requires me to do two opposite things at the same time. First, I must bow my head. This honors the Jewish tradition of seeing scholarship as a holy calling—or as I view scholarship, as an apostolic vocation ("An hour of study, for a modern apostle, is an hour of prayer"[9]). Bowing my head is a discipline of thankfulness. Mother loved to harangue us with "You can't say 'thank you' enough." Nothing makes us more human than our ability to say, "Thank you." Nothing makes us more inhuman than our forgetfulness to say, "Thank you." The bending down to enter my study forces me to bow in humility, remembering Paul's warning that "knowledge puffs up while love builds up."[10] My bowed prayer as I enter my study is "Lord, don't let me get puffy and bloated. Give your church a taut body, a taught mind, and a sinewy spirit. Amen."

But at the same time I bow down to enter my octagonally shaped inner sanctum, I have to step up about six inches, or I trip over the threshold. The design of my door frame forces me to be both humble and confident at the same time. To embark on the grand apostolic adventure of scholarship and writing, I must bow down to the Lord, and I must step up in faith, setting my sails to catch the Spirit as I open the Scriptures.

A "right spirit" involves this kind of confidence and humility, a step-up sense of importance ("I can do all things") and a bow-down sense of impotence ("Without [Christ] you can do nothing").[11]

# 18

# GRANDFATHER'S CHAIR

⎯⎯⎯⎯⎯ ❧ ⎯⎯⎯⎯⎯

*It is not what we give to Jesus, it's what*
*we fail to give that is wasted.*

MABEL BOGGS SWEET

I never met my grandfather Ira Sweet, but I was named
after him.[1] Ira was a glove cutter who cut and sewed
leather. He only got to eighth grade, but he proudly wore a
white shirt and tie to work every day. All glove cutters did.
They were the aristocrats of the glove industry, following in
the tradition of Yahweh God, who "made leather clothing"
for Adam and Eve.[2] Paul's "tent-making" profession was
really sewing leather for tents—a divine profession, as we
are all called to be needle-and-thread tent-makers for the
habitation of God among us.

Dad's mother, Ida Sweet (both my grandmothers were
named Ida), died when he was eighteen, and two years

later, on 10 March 1934, when Ira Sweet was fifty-seven, he married May Fancher, ten years his junior, in the living room of the Free Methodist parsonage of Rev. C. A. Steucke. Witnesses to the wedding were my father's sister Charlotte and her husband, Howard Schemerhorn. After a week's honeymoon, Ira and May resided at 50 North Street, across the street from where Aunt Charlotte lived. Shortly thereafter they moved to 74 Orchard Street, which is now an empty lot.

The glove industry had its ups and downs. For example, in 1940 Ira spent four and a half months looking for work. During that time my father supported the family with his salary as a bookkeeper, while Gramma May did piecework sewing from her home to bring in some income. When Ira did work full time, the days were long—often twelve-hour shifts (five to five), five to six days a week.

When Ira came home, he had a ritual. After supper, he would sit down in a homemade kitchen chair and read theology. He loved books on eschatology, archaeology, and holiness theology. He loved books on B. T. Roberts and the Free Methodist movement and faithfully tithed to the local Free Methodist Church.[3] When times were lean, Ira would personally solicit the businesspeople in Gloversville for money to buy coal for the church.

Because he was so short, Ira put his feet on the lower rung of the chair rather than the floor. While reading he restlessly rotated his right foot up and down so that it wore down a wafer-thin indentation in the horizontal bar. Every book he owned he signed in the front, and when he finished reading a book, he inserted the date in the back. You knew his favorite books by the multiple insertions of dates.

This plain kitchen chair, and some of his books, are among my most prized possessions. When I look at the chair, which is now in my study, I think to myself, *This is what a lifetime of scholarship looks like; this is what a lifetime of theological reflection looks like; this is what a tent-making ministry looks like.* I am not an academic theologian or a professional theologian, with primary allegiances to the guild. I am a church theologian, a semiotic theologian, a motion theologian like my namesake, Ira Sweet, who worked as a glove cutter by day and a theologian by night.

# 19

# GLOVER'S MANGE CURE

*Jesus enters no problem he is not invited into.*

MABEL BOGGS SWEET

Mother insisted her boys wear their "Sunday best" to church. This culture no longer has the sacrament of "Sunday clothes," although we lose at our peril the daily need to clothe ourselves in Sunday sacraments. But Saturday was the day of getting ready for Sunday, which featured two imperatives: a bath (our five-square-foot bathroom had no shower) and a weekly shampoo with Glover's Mange Cure.

Our Sunday hair had the fragrance of tar. There was nothing that smelled so foul or looked so vile as this shampoo. My brothers and I were never told why our hair had to go through the torture of a treatment made for dogs, wolves, sheep, and bears. Later we found out that this was Mother's prophylactic exercise in protecting us from the diseases of our neighborhood: lice, mites, scabies, and demodicosis. All we knew at the time was that when Mother shampooed our hair with this nauseating liquid, there was no scrubbing gently of the scalp. No matter our squeals of "Ma, that hurts," Mother gave scalp rub-downs when she washed our head with Glover's Mange Cure.

I stopped asking why I couldn't use a shampoo like everyone else uses or why my scalp had to be massaged and scraped with something I could never tell anyone about. I knew by heart the lectures such a question would trigger. One was about why I shouldn't care or compare myself to anyone else. "As for me and my household, we will serve the LORD."[1] What the Lord had to do with Glover's Mange Cure was never made clear.

The second lecture I got was "Whatever you do, put everything you have in it. Do it with all your might." If you gave your word to do something, then you owed that something your best, and you made the best of that something. Why settle for a bath to be just a bath when your outward washing could be a ritual that symbolizes inward cleansing and soul purification? Glover's Mange Cure may have been my first introduction to semiotics.

Other phrases Mother threw at our protests were "Idle hands are the devil's workshop" or "We hear that some among you are idle and disruptive. They are not busy; they are busybodies."[2] Or most succinctly, "No work, no eat." If Wittgenstein said that philosophers should hail one another by saying, "Take your time," in Mother's mind disciples of

Jesus would better greet each other with "Redeem the time" or "Keep moving." God is a God who is always active. It is part of our mission to keep up with God's motion and movement. Even baptismal waters should be not still but moving, Mother believed. To this day I order "sparkling water," never "still water." Mother also reminded us of the words Jesus spoke when he knew his own death was near: "As long as day lasts I must carry out the work of the one who sent me; the night will soon be here when no one can work."[3]

One of the greatest challenges for a script writer is to turn a great novelist's work into a film. In the early 1950s, a script writer was working with Roman Catholic novelist Graham Greene (1904–1991). If Greene's mind was momentarily blank, you didn't know what he might write. Or rather, you did know. "You're a bit like a British documentary," the screenwriter accused Greene, annoyed by the tapping of Greene's pencil. "When they are in any doubt, they cut to sea gulls; in your case, you cut immediately to God. Can we please avoid cutting to God?"[4]

Whether it was shampoo or Winnie the Pooh, Mother always cut to Jesus. Too many sermons spare nothing except the main point—that God spared nothing, even his Son, to show us how much God loves us.

In one of Mother's sermons, she flipped what Jesus said to Peter in Mark 8—"Who do you say I am?"—upside down. Instead she asked, "Who does Jesus say we are?" To a politician you are a voter. To an advertiser you are a consumer. To a government you are a social security number. To your employer you are a paycheck. But to God, who alone sees you as you, you are

- ❖ ambassadors for Christ (2 Corinthians 5:20)
- ❖ believers (Acts 14:1)
- ❖ the body of Christ (Romans 12:5; 1 Corinthians 12:27; Colossians 1:18)
- ❖ brothers (Matthew 23:8; Acts 14:2)
- ❖ children of God (John 1:12; 11:52; Romans 8:16)
- ❖ citizens (Ephesians 2:19)
- ❖ disciples (Acts 6:1; 20:1; 21:16)
- ❖ followers of the Way (Acts 9:2; 22:4; 24:14)
- ❖ friends (John 15:14-15)
- ❖ heirs of God and fellow heirs with Christ (Romans 8:17)
- ❖ letters from Christ (2 Corinthians 3:3)
- ❖ light (Matthew 5:14; Ephesians 5:8-9)
- ❖ martyrs of Jesus (Revelation 17:6)
- ❖ ministers of God (2 Corinthians 6:4)
- ❖ new creatures (2 Corinthians 5:17)
- ❖ the Israel of God (Galatians 6:16)
- ❖ the image of Christ (Romans 8:29)
- ❖ part of God's household (Ephesians 2:19)
- ❖ recipients of gifts (Ephesians 4:11-12; Romans 12:6-8)
- ❖ saints (Acts 9:32)
- ❖ salt (Matthew 5:13)
- ❖ sheep of the fold (John 10:3)
- ❖ sons (Galatians 4:5; Hebrews 12:7)

- ❖ stewards (1 Corinthians 4:1-2; 1 Peter 4:10)
- ❖ strangers and nomads (Hebrews 11:13-16)
- ❖ temples of the Holy Spirit (1 Corinthians 6:19-20)
- ❖ witnesses (John 15:27; Acts 1:8)

I sensed some other things in the fury of Mother's scrubbing. First, there was a rush against time. Life whizzes by faster and faster as you age, and dusk seems to come around every fifteen minutes. Mother never perjured herself to say one positive thing about aging. She was constantly warning us of how short life was, how precious and fragile its gift, and how we must make every day count for something.

When Picasso tried, in 1905, to paint his now-famous portrait of Gertrude Stein, he struggled and failed in the course of some eighty sittings to capture her likeness. Eventually he gave up and went off for a holiday in Spain, where he encountered African art and fell in love with the art of the primitive ceremonial mask. On his return to Paris, he dispensed entirely with Stein as a live model, completing the portrait, in her absence, with mask-like features. When Gertrude Stein finally saw it, she didn't think it looked like her. To this the artist observed, "In the end she will manage to look just like it."[5] Time proved him right.

The scrubbing ritual was also a releasing of pent-up frustration and a grieving over Mother's lost future. Samuel Johnson called bereavement "a whole system of hopes, and designs, and expectations . . . swept away at once, and nothing left but bottomless vacuity."[6] Grief is complex, encompassing hopes and designs, dreams lost and aches gained, the traumas of the past, and the traumas of the future.

Strangely enough, the 1998 movie *Saving Private Ryan* helped me to understand the Glover's Mange Cure ritual. It is in part the story about General George Marshall's decision to bring the fourth son of a grieving mother—her only remaining son—back from the front during World War II. Whatever it takes: Find him and bring him home. But the other part of the story is about the struggle of a squad and its captain (a high school English teacher, husband, and father) to carry out their assignment. At the end, with Private Ryan saved at the cost of many lives, the captain lies before him dying. His last words: "Earn this."

In her frantic scrubbing of her boys in prophylactic antiseptic, Mother was saying, "I've sacrificed everything for you boys. Now earn this."

Sometimes "the burning of the noontide heat and the burdens of the day"[7] take the oxygen away. As kids we never knew the toll it took on Mother to lose her ordination, raise three boys, buck up a sickly and depressed husband, and fight with church authorities over the meaning of "worldliness." She was ostracized by local churches, shunned by her husband's family, surrounded by children in need of constant monitoring, without intellectual stimulation or feedback, stripped of a network of friends, and surrounded by needy acquaintances who made her life meaningful but always wielded her Southern heritage against her. She felt isolated in every way—personally, intellectually, culturally, professionally, and relationally—and the worst torture is solitary confinement. (She also had a serious thyroid condition that today would most likely be diagnosed as Graves' disease.)

The depths of Mother's loneliness and depression only became evident as I was researching this book and found, folded and tucked away in her Bible, a bombshell of a letter. It was a farewell note to her boys, in the hopes that one day we would understand that what she was about to do was because she loved us so much. Whether it was a suicide note or a running-away note, I'll never be sure. Why she kept it will forever be a mystery. The note was hidden in a file of newspaper clippings, some from the 1950s, most from the 1960s. Maybe she struggled with depression all her life, and we missed it. Maybe that is why my aunts Jean and Patsy at various times moved into our home when we were growing up. I thought at the time we were doing favors to these "maiden aunts," expanding their exposure to potential suitors. But maybe they were sent by Gramma and Granddad to help Mother through her dark valleys.

Some things you never get over; you just move on. I know firsthand how something someone told me years ago can return like a tide to swamp my spirit. The haunting effect and chronic stress of what the hierarchies of two denominations said about Mother and stripped away from her can only be guessed. And to my everlasting shame, my rebellious nature did not make things any easier on her.

What kept Mother from acting on her note? I have asked myself that question a hundred times since I found it. My best answer is her scattered sayings still resounding in my head, words that stitch together to form a breastplate of armor:

* We are not our own.
* "You were bought at a price."[8]
* We do not belong to ourselves. We belong to God. We are God's children. So we guard the life that does not belong to us but has been entrusted to us as we guard the life of one of our children, or any child.
* Life is not ours to dispose of.

It perplexed me why French Catholic mystic Madame Guyon (1648–1717) was one of Mother's favorite people to quote. Then I learned her story of persecution by the church, and I understood better. But I most fully understood when I found this quotation highlighted and hand-copied in one of Mother's notebooks: "If you dare the spiritual pilgrimage, you need to remember in times of calamity, and in times of what appear to be dry spells, and in that time which men will call a spiritual winter: Life is there."

Perhaps all these forces collaborated in my subconscious to give me, for as long as I can remember, a tender spot in my heart for those who take their own life, including those six people who took their own lives in the Bible: Samson, Saul and his armor-bearer, Ahithophel, the Israelite king Zimri, and Judas Iscariot. I believe suicide victims will be met by Jesus personally at the gate. He will embrace each one and say, "Son/Daughter, you found it a little too much for you, didn't you?"

# 20

# POTLUCKS

<hr />

*Who wants to get to a man's heart through his stomach?*
*Who wants someone who loves to eat, not loves to live?*

MABEL BOGGS SWEET

My brothers and I were born with "Boggs appetites" and cast-iron stomachs. At one point Mother took me to the doctor to see if I had something wrong with me (I was sure it was a tapeworm). I was 6'4", 144 pounds, and ate four sandwiches at a time without getting full. (In my defense, each sandwich only had one slice of bologna on it.)

To ward off any embarrassment, Mother implemented three strategies. First, she insisted the Sweet family be last in line at any public meal. Second, she always fed us before we went to potluck suppers at the church. Third, she gave us a story.

First, the back of the line. Mother used to say, "Boys,

don't live to eat, eat to live." I since learned it was Socrates who first said, "Worthless people live only to eat and drink; people of worth eat and drink only to live." We were not to flaunt our hunger, no matter how hungry we were. And besides, we wouldn't want God to see us rushing to the front of the line. Mother made Kant's categorical imperative—to behave as if that behavior should be universal law—into a daily calendar imperative: Behave as if your deeds could be seen by all, since the all-seeing eye of God is watching. (We didn't need a dollar bill to be reminded of God's all-seeing eye. It didn't sit atop a pyramid, but atop everything we did.) Would the world be better if God universalized what I'm about to do? What if the whole world rushed to the front of the line?

The prefeeding ritual was accompanied by the warning: "Don't do anything to embarrass your mother. Don't do anything to embarrass your name. Always remember your name is S-W-E-E-T."

When the father of an employee thanked S. Truett Cathy, founder and longtime chair of Chick-fil-A, for hiring his son, Cathy supposedly replied, "Your son represents me well." Similarly, Mother expected her boys to "represent the Sweet name well," in the hopes that each one of us would one day hear Jesus say, "Len/Phil/John represents me well."

When I was growing up, much time was spent on the mark of the beast. What is it? Do you have it? Would you ever get it? But forget the mark of the beast. Do you bear the Maker's mark? For example, do people become better when they are in your presence? Do people feel inches taller after talking to you? Each one of us has such a Maker's mark. Mother wanted us to find it and wear it.

Finally, in preparation for potlucks Mother ritually related the story of a salesman who shared a meal at a customer's home. There were six boys in the home, and the salesman noticed that the older boys always picked the bigger portions, leaving the dregs to the littlest boy. After a couple of meals with the family and watching this grabfest play itself out again and again, the salesman brought a special gift the next time he sat down at the table with the family. He placed a half-dozen apples in a bowl for everyone to share. Sure enough, the older brothers snapped up the bigger apples, leaving the littlest lad with the smallest apple. When the lad bit into his apple, however, his teeth hit something very hard. When he pulled out what was in his apple, he found a $100 gold piece.

After Mother told that story, my brothers and I started fighting over who would get the smallest portions.

# 21

# CHOCOLATE ÉCLAIRS

―⸙―

*If God cannot bless what I am doing I must stop my doings.*
MABEL BOGGS SWEET

As soon as I reached the age when it was allowed, I had a morning paper route. Every morning I would get up at 4 a.m. and deliver papers before school. During some of the winters, when we got two hundred inches of snow and the blizzard conditions were brutal, Mother would get up with me and drive me for part of the route.

Saturday morning was usually reserved for making the rounds to collect the money, the profits of which Mother allowed us to keep. We never got an allowance for chores. But we were allowed to keep the money we made, with the expectation that we would save it for college.

I saved some of it, but I spent money on books and

clothes. And on Saturday mornings, after I delivered the papers, I would treat myself to a pastry at Feldman's Bakery. This local pastry shop had hard rolls and every pastry you could imagine, but no bread. They didn't sell bread. I would stand in front of the window, waiting for them to open, and stare at all the macaroons and madeleines, meringue tarts, Neapolitan cookies, and fancy things I couldn't afford. I learned their names, imagined them in my mouth, and said to myself, *One day*.

When they finally opened the store I would be the first one in, rewarding myself with a chocolate éclair, the one that squirted vanilla cream (not whipped cream) out the sides and ends. To this day my image of heaven is a library with a patisserie in the reading room. The door of heaven's House of Bread, the ultimate pastry palace, is standing open, but we keep trying to break in the back door because we don't understand, in George Orwell's famous revamp of Ecclesiastes: "Using your loaf won't fill your breadbin" (or "You can't have your cake and eat it too").

Mother believed in hard work and the ethic of work. The only letter to the editor she ever wrote was a letter about the value of hard work, citing a quotation attributed to Thomas Jefferson: "The democracy will cease to exist when you take away from those who are willing to work and give to those who would not." If Jesus could say, "My Father is always at his work . . . and I too am working,"[1] how could we not be part of God's continual creative activity in the world? One of the rare moments when I felt Mother was truly proud of me was when she quoted my colleague and friend Daryl Ward: "To work with Len Sweet you need twenty-four hours a day."

Mother was always on the lookout for those who needed help and would drop anything she was doing to reach out her hand. The church, as she put it, ought to be focused more on the needs of "bums" than "bishops." Or to flip the metaphor, to continue Jesus' mission on earth is to do more than uplift those already "sitting with their bums in the butter." As poet Bertolt Brecht wrote, "Justice is the bread of the people":

*As daily bread is necessary*
*So is daily justice.*
*It is even necessary several times a day.*[2]

Mother had a Chekhovian ear for the hidden semiotic moment and showed an amazing capacity for what the French call *disponibilité*, or what Mother called Jesus' "bless-your-heart-and-gizzard" attentiveness. In the midst of fulfilling his mission, Jesus was always *disponible*, able to be interrupted, constantly available and responsive to his context and the needs of the moment, yet undeterred and undetoured in his larger mission. To pay attention, in Hebrew, is *lasim lev*—literally, to "put heart." The deep listening and instant intimacy of *disponibilité* is an act of love.

Mother showed this same *disponibilité*, although her "deep listening" could take some strange expressions. With others' kids, it could take the form of "Duck Duck Goose" yard games. With strangers, Mother would befriend them at the most difficult time of their lives. With us, the temperature could plunge and a north wind blow through the room in an instant when she went into *disponibilité*. She could also slam on the brakes, stop the car, and stare at beauty, in or out of the car, and not be embarrassed by what anyone behind or around her was thinking. (Of course, my brothers and I were horrified and humiliated, looking around to see if anyone recognized us as we slunk down as far as we could in the car.)

Mother had no use for a gospel that wasn't "social." Any "gospel" that wasn't social wasn't gospel. Yet to be more obsessed with the "social" than the "gospel" was to fail at both. Only Jesus saves. Evil is real. And some people will choose not to be saved and to do evil. Mother had no use for the notion, as Leonard Bernstein put it in *West Side Story*, that people's bad behavior can be chalked up to purely social causes.[3] We all are "bad people" whom Jesus wants to make good, if only we will let him.

Only one of the two thieves at Calvary was saved. As Vladimir put it in *Waiting for Godot*, "It's a reasonable percentage."[4]

# 22

# THE WRINGER

*Jesus never gave an altar call. . . . Unless Matthew 11:28*
*could be called an altar call: "Come to me, all of you who are*
*weary and carry heavy burdens, and I will give you rest."*

MABEL BOGGS SWEET

I am a natal Christian, a new convert. The road away from Christianity became for me the road back to Christ.

Some people come to faith easy. Some people come to faith hard. I was one of the hard ones. I was not an easy believer. I was a hard study. Rebellion runs in my veins and rushes through my brain. I went through the wringer, and I put my parents through the wringer.

Whether my rebellious nature was a coincidence or consequence of being a child of a powerful and frustrated mother is a matter for you to decide. But it is a rebellious nature that began to bring me back to the church, as I saw how faith itself could be a gesture of defiance, an act of revolution. At my lowest point in life, I refused to believe in nothing, and I fought back.

Very early in life, my brothers and I learned that a good percentage of life is chores. One does the chores so that one can get to the creative stuff. Clothes washing was divided up into three parts: One of us (usually Phil) put the clothes into the washer and through the wringer; one of us (usually John) took the basket of clothes to the three lines that ran the length of our thin side yard and hung the wet apparel on the lines with wooden and plastic clothespins; I usually took down the dry clothes from the line and ironed everything. We were among the last to know the fun of playing hide-and-seek between lines of drying clothes, the sound and feel of frozen jeans dancing in the winter wind, the smell of sun-dried pillowcases against your cheek.

---

*Lord, may my prayers be so much in Your will that You may be able to get glory to Your name. May my living be so led by You until Your plan shall be accomplished in my life. This I pray for each of my boys.*

MABEL BOGGS SWEET,
PRAYER, 17 APRIL 1979

---

Each member of the family knew firsthand what it's like to go through the wringer. My rebellious nature put every member of the family through that wringer in one way or another. My first seventeen years of life I lived the Christian faith through the loins and lens of my parents, mainly Mother. But when I was seventeen, I dramatically deconverted.

I wish I had a deconversion story worthy of Augustine, but I don't. Augustine was brought up by a Christian mother (Monica) in the hills of Numidia, now eastern Algeria. He was deconverted by reading Cicero's *Hortensius* and finding the literary and moral standards of Cicero superior to what he found in the Scriptures—for example, polygamy in Genesis and differing genealogies in the Gospels. But he could not shake off the faith of his mother, and eventually he reconnected to Christianity.

I don't have a testimony that glorious, but I can date my deconversion down to the song and verse and one particular never-to-be-forgotten moment of decision. I was playing the organ for the "Great Preaching" Sunday morning worship that concluded the eight-day Pine Grove camp meeting that the Genesee Conference of the Free Methodist Church conducted each year at Saratoga Springs, New York. In the front row sat Linda, the girl I was dating. I thought I was pretty hot stuff, and I couldn't wait until the end of the invitation song to get what I thought would be my good-bye kiss.

On the third of six verses of the invitational hymn "Softly and Tenderly," out of the corner of my eye I saw Mother's best friend Ruth get out of her seat toward the back of the tabernacle and "hit the sawdust trail," as they used to call it. I couldn't believe my eyes. Ruth Kuhn was the closest thing I knew to a saint, next to Mother. She was the one I called on the phone when I feared that the Rapture had taken place: If she answered, I would quickly hang up and breathe a big sigh of relief, knowing that we had not been left behind. (To this day I am tender toward hang-ups—you never know who is calling and hanging up, and why.) Ruth, the person on whom I banked all my eschatological hopes, was making her way up to the altar. But then she kept going, coming right up to me. She threw herself on me and got medieval: "Now is your appointed time, Lenny! Now is your time!" She began pulling me off the organ bench onto the altar below.

What's the worst thing that can happen to a seventeen-year-old? Especially one who is dating the district super-intendent's daughter? At first I tried ignoring Ruth, hoping she'd go away. I had years of practice ignoring pulls at heart-strings. "I shall not be moved" was my theme song growing up, my fingers rooted in the back of the pew, while listening to the yammering and sometimes hammering of the most heart-wrenching altar calls ever given.

The cold shoulder wasn't working on Ruth, so I tried reasoning with her. "If I were to go to the altar with you, Ruth, who would play the organ? We'd have to end the service."

Her entreaties only became louder: "The Lord will provide, Lenny. You just go. The Lord will send angels to play in your place. Now is your appointed time!"

I tried shoo-shooing her away. But the more I tried to push Ruth away, the more determined she was to haul me to the altar. We slowly came to the end of "Softly and Tenderly," and no one had come to the altar. All eyes were fixed on the drama at the organ. The preacher leaned over the pulpit and spoke softly to the congregation: "Obviously the Lord is at work here this morning. We must give the Spirit plenty of time to work. Let's sing this song one more time. All the verses, please."

That's when it hit me: *You're playing for your own altar call!*

Ruth kept wailing and wrenching me off the bench. I kept playing and singing inside, "I shall, I shall, I shall not be moved." The harder she pulled, the louder I played and inwardly sang. When we arrived at the third verse, she suddenly stopped. She shook herself off, turned around, and retraced her steps back to her seat. About a third of the way down the center aisle, she stopped, hung her head, and shook it emphatically a couple of times.

When I saw that shake of her head, I knew the semiotics of what that meant. Ruth was symbolically releasing me to the devil. In her mind I had quenched the Spirit, the one unpardonable sin, and from now on I was on my own, with no protection from God.

When I saw her do that, I said to myself, *I'm out of here. I no longer believe there is a God, but if you do exist, God, I hate you. I want nothing to do with you.* That was the moment of my deconversion, my faith-toppling moment—during my own altar call.

There are thresholds we can cross. We have a language of never-agains which demonstrate this:

- "That's one time too many."
- "You've pushed me on too far."
- "You went over the line this time."
- "I've had it up to here."
- "That's the last straw."

The shaking of the head pushed me over the threshold.

When Mother came up to me afterward, it was as if I had contracted coprolalia or Tourette's syndrome. I couldn't stop swearing; I spewed out every swear word I had ever heard but never uttered. For those present, my flood of filth just confirmed the verdict of the shaking head.

I never saw or heard from Linda again.

Some people plant wild oats. For the next six years I planted a prairie. I became an atheist who told people—even told God—that I didn't believe in God.

The irony was that it was only after my deconversion that God started working on me big-time. I was no longer talking to God through my parents. I was talking to God directly. I was now engaged in a conversation, and that conversation was the beginning of a relationship that has brought me to where I am today. What does God want more than anything from us? A relationship. And even an argumentative and negative relationship is better than rote and ritual obedience.

The minute I deconverted, I began a very passionate and personal quest to determine what was truth with a capital T. I went on pilgrimages, visiting Marx and Mao, Buddha and Krishna, rock and pop, Eastern religions and no religion. As an apostate reprobate, that impenitent thief on the cross was one of my heroes, my patron saint, even: defiant, glacial, impermeable.

To say I broke Mother's heart with my rifts, ructions, and rebellions would be an understatement. My rejection of faith was a double blow: Because of her gender, she could not fulfill her mission, but I could. It hit me one day what was at stake for Mother: Sometimes she would break down and let me know how hard she was praying for me. "If I don't," she said with fear in her eyes, "I may never see you again."

In college I double-majored in psychology and history. I wasn't sure whether I would go to graduate school to become a psychologist or a historian. I finally decided that history better explains psychology than psychology explains history. I also reasoned that if religion is true, its study tells us a great deal about the nature of God, and if religion is false, its study tells us a great deal about the nature of humanity. Either way, it is worth scholarly attention. I was trying to figure out the historical background of my upbringing and why it was the way it was from an intellectual standpoint. It felt like I had been mugged, and I needed to learn everything I could about the mugger and the mugging. So I enrolled simultaneously in a PhD program in history and an MDiv in church history. My doctoral mentor, Winthrop S. Hudson, thought I would be more likely to find a teaching position in a seminary than in a university.

There were four reasons why I chose the two graduate schools in Rochester, New York.

First, I went to the University of Rochester for my PhD because of the providence of almighty God; that is to say, the school gave me a scholarship and paid my tuition. Except for my brother John, who never knew a "B" grade existed and scored in the SAT and GRE stratospheres, we Sweet boys chose schools not on the basis of where we wanted to study but on the basis of who offered the most scholarships.

Second, even though a Methodist-related school offered more money, my undergraduate history professor W. Harrison Daniel, whom I trusted, suggested that Baptist historian Winthrop S. Hudson in Rochester would be the best mentor for me.

Third, the newly formed cluster of seminaries in Rochester (Colgate Rochester/Bexley Hall/Crozer/St.Bernards) was appealing because Crozer was where Martin Luther King Jr. had studied before he went to Boston University for his doctorate. Think of all the stories I could learn from those who taught him there.

Finally, the seminary was known as one of two "death-of-God" seminaries (the other being Candler School of Theology at Emory University). Death-of-God theologian Bill Hamilton was no longer there; he had fled to New College in Sarasota, Florida, and then to Portland State

University after death threats pummeled him and his family when he was featured in the 8 April 1966 cover story of *Time* magazine, and then four months later in *Playboy* magazine amid pictures of a topless Jane Fonda. If I were to go to a seminary in my unbelieving state, I thought it only appropriate that it be a death-of-God seminary. (I knew that Nietzsche was the source of the phrase "God is dead," and he got it from one of Martin Luther's hymns, where he talked about how God also died mystically and theologically when Jesus died on the cross.[1])

The key component of every liminality, as anthropologist Victor Turner noted, is that river water that has become murky wetlands or swampy streams keeps tracking with the river. In liminal stages of life, you need to leave the main river so that the toxins can get removed and the water cleansed. But all the while that purifying process is taking place, you must keep tracking alongside the river so that you can return to it. And when you return to the river, you enter it with a higher degree of passion and purity than when you left it.

That was what happened to me. During my six years of atheism, I stayed connected with Christianity in a unique "tracking." I said, "I'm no longer in that river," but I kept engaging it, musically and intellectually.

Because my parents provided no financial help for my brothers and me to go to college, except for one $1,000 check (the total amount Dad had saved for our entire college education), we all were dependent on scholarships, financial aid, and employment. One of the ways I earned money was to provide my services as an organist for worship and special services like weddings and funerals. So every week, guess where I was on Sunday? In church, interacting with God's people and listening to sermons and the hymnody of the church. And at least one other time a week, guess where I was? In church, playing for a wedding or funeral and connecting with the saints. I couldn't escape God even if I had tried, and I couldn't escape the soundtrack of the church. That's how God kept me in relationship, a relationship that was being cleansed and purified even when I didn't know it. Besides, what distinguishes a house of theology most of all are not its tenets but its tenants.

The second way I kept "tracking" with the church was intellectually. During my seminary education, I had a requirement of field education, meaning I had to work in a church setting. My major faculty mentor invited me to be his teaching assistant so I wouldn't have to do church work. But the dean of students, a chain-smoking Episcopal priest named Joseph A. Pelham (1930–1992), vetoed the exception. My mentor took the veto as a slap in the face and got the whole faculty to pass a resolution against forcing me to work in a church. Again Dean Pelham vetoed it!

So there I was, headed to a Presbyterian church for supervised ministry when I wanted nothing to do with the church. I was not happy, but I wanted my A, so I had to do what I was assigned. A marvelous pastor, C. Frederick Yoos, helped me fall in love with Jesus and the church again. He was a wonderful preacher, a fantastic pastor, and a skilled mentor. Under his tutelage and that of a Lutheran campus pastor, Fred Lassen (1940–2007), who went from Geneseo to be campus pastor at Oberlin College, I saw how the church is the sleeping giant of our time—the most underrated power for good in the world today.

Our heads want to know God, but our hearts want to be known by God. The more my head was buzzing, the more my heart was growing in its desires.

One day Pastor Yoos sent me on a blind pastoral call to someone in need. I had no idea what I would find. He just told me I was going to have to handle it pastorally. I was sent to the home of Margey Wilke, and I found her crying when she answered the door. It was the anniversary of her husband's death in Vietnam. I had a number of friends who had been killed or maimed there, and it suddenly hit me that Margey's husband could have been me. But for the grace of God I could have been killed in Vietnam. Why was I still alive, when so many I knew weren't?

As I started to minister to Margey, she ministered to me. And I ended my first "pastoral call" on my knees in her living room, asking God to forgive me and for Christ to come into my life.

Before I deconverted, I was nominally a disciple. I was living a religion through my parents. I had a hand-faith, a faith that went through all the motions but had no head and no heart. It is now clear to me that I had to go away in order to come back.

That's the definition of liminality. Though it looked as if I were moving away from God, I found myself moving closer to God. It is important for parents of adolescents to remember: Sometimes people appear to be on a fight-or-flight pattern in their faith, but it can be because God is most at work in their life. We just have to be patient. When I deconverted from Christianity, paradoxically, I was on my way to Christianity. I got there by way of agnosticism, atheism, Marxism, academicism, religious studies-ism, and pluralism. My "planting a prairie" was an intellectual furrowing of the ground.

I love people who are arguing with God the loudest. Often "Here I am" (*Hineni*) comes after a bout of "Leave me alone." That's the case with Noah, Abraham, Moses, Samuel, Isaiah, Jeremiah . . . It's a perilous thing to say *Hineni*. But as Adam and Jonah found out, it's even more perilous to refuse to say *Hineni*.

My faith was planted as a seed by my parents. They really wanted to plant a whole potted plant, but I ripped that out with my deconversion. What remained planted was the seed. And that seed was watered by the prayers of my parents and the ministries of many preachers and laypeople. I would not be here today without the nudgings and nurturings of my upbringing, even when I resisted all nudge and nurture. Organic evangelism needs time to grow, and as one of Mother's favorite sayings went, "God's clock keeps perfect time."

# 23

# MATCHBOXES AND SAWDUST

*Holy Ghost appointments have Holy Ghost conclusions.*
MABEL BOGGS SWEET

Much of human memory is governed by smells—in my case, the odor of mashed pitch and pulp in the paper-mill town of Covington, Virginia;[1] the aroma of old books at the Library of Congress and, across the street, coffee and hot cross buns; and the coconut-scented beaches of South Wellfleet, Massachusetts.[2] I became a historian because of the romance of the reading room at the Library of Congress, which became for me a holy place. But the two dominant smells of my growing-up years were the smells of heaven and hell: the burning matchboxes of our bathrooms and the sawdust of camp meetings.

We couldn't afford room sprays or deodorizers, so

Mother used matches to mask smells generated in the bathroom. Since my father got free matches at the bank and had quite a stash of matches from military bases (many of them now quite valuable to collectors), Mother usually had displayed for use a carton of matchboxes, one whole matchbox per flush. With one bathroom and five people, something was always burning. And how much my brothers and I loved to light a whole box of matches and then swoosh the sulfurous smoke throughout the small space.

Mother treated our colds by mixing Vicks VapoRub (camphor, menthol, and eucalyptus oil) in a pot of hot water and making us inhale the steam. It smelled good, but it also cleared out our sinuses. To this day I love Jack Black Shampoo for its eucalyptus smell.[3] But my favorite shampoos are balsam scented (for example, Nordic Wood by Philip B), because some of my most wonderful memories of growing up took place at Pine Grove Camp Meeting outside Saratoga Springs, New York. When I open balsam shampoo and sniff its boreal fragrance, I have opened a chest full of camp meeting memories, releasing into my life the smell of family, home-cooked meals, sawdust trails, shouting Methodists, teenage dates, and furtive kisses behind brush arbors. Fragrance is the fifth dimension of faith.

With what "oyster-like tenacity" (Nathaniel Hawthorne's phrase)[4] we cling to emotionally charged places! In my life the most emotionally charged place was the camp meeting—old-time, backwoods, calico religion with long tables and short stories (well, sometimes not so short).

As a product of the holiness tradition, I had the privilege of experiencing firsthand both of the two Protestant pilgrimages. The first is the family reunion, especially in its Southern form. The second is the journey to a sacred space, most often an ancestral church, cemetery, or meeting ground. For me the two came together in a Pilgrim Holiness camp meeting outside Albany called Victory Grove Camp and in the Free Methodist Pine Grove Camp. Both the family reunion and the sacred grounds were found for the Sweet family in the yearly pilgrimages to these two camp meetings.

Camp meetings arose among the plain folk on the southwestern frontier, but they soon spread everywhere. First called "brush arbor revivals," "tent meetings," "protracted meetings," or "open-air cathedrals," by the early days of the nineteenth century the name "camp meetings" had stuck. From the very beginning, camp meetings exhibited pronounced emotionalism and bizarre behavior. This is partly because camp meetings were forms of male evangelism, out-of-doors settings where men could let their emotions out without fear of being ridiculed or seen as unmanly. And when emotions long pent up are permitted out, one can never predict or control what comes next. Camp meetings were the one place where men were free to "pump your peepers," an old camp-meeting expression for when sermons were so moving and touching that one could not help but cry.

Virginia Baptists held camp meetings as early as 1767,

but camp meetings were not brought to the evangelical world's attention until 1799 on a Kentucky frontier. There, legendary meetings at Red River in 1799, at Gaspar River in 1800, and most famously at Cane Ridge in 1801—under Methodist, Presbyterian, and Baptist auspices—brought camp meetings to the forefront of USAmerica's religious consciousness, where they would remain as evangelical expressions of popular religious piety until the mid-1940s. Unprecedented crowds of ten thousand to twenty-five thousand were matched by spectacular conversions of notorious drunkards, criminals, prostitutes, and disbelievers, not to mention the emotional spectacles of the "exercises" (falling, drinking, barking, dancing, and laughing) and "impressions" (marriage, business, and health).

Such goings-on scared away many evangelicals. By 1805 the Baptists and Presbyterians drew back from sponsoring camp meetings, leaving them to the Methodists both to defend (as Lorenzo Dow, who introduced camp meetings into England in 1807, did so systematically in his *History of Cosmopolite*) and to develop (as they did with great success, with six hundred camp meetings held in 1816 and one thousand in 1820).

The first Methodist bishop, Francis Asbury, demonstrated his enthusiasm for camp meetings when he chronicled the numbers saved and sanctified at an 1806 camp meeting in a letter to one of his presiding elders. Asbury concluded with the remark, "Oh, my brother, when all our quarterly meetings become campmeetings, and 1,000 souls should be converted, our American millennium will begin."[5] Not until Methodists demonstrated that emotions could be wiped cleaner through religious expressions at camp meetings did other evangelical denominations begin to participate in them again.

Camp meetings were a favorite target for popular literature, especially novels, where sarcasm and criticism of camp meetings often came to a head. There was not a dearth of material for critics to work with. Apart from what contemporaries called the "religious catalepsy," there was the phenomenon of mixed motives with which people came to camp meetings. Some women came for the dress parade and cooking showdowns; some wealthy people came to pawn their power; some politicians came to seek votes; some merchants came to hawk wares; some town rowdies came to stir up trouble; some whiskey peddlers came with more than cider in their canteens; and some young people came for reasons which are best not to scrutinize too closely. I know I got my first introduction to pole dancers at a camp meeting, as one of the bonnet babes (also known as "vestal virgins") got so "happy" she did a Jesus jig and sanctified stomp around the tent post.

Perhaps camp meetings fell under the greatest suspicion, however, for their mixing of business with pleasure. In the words of a character in Mary Clemmer Ames's 1871 novel *Eirene*, "The whole scene bore witness to what it was—a great religious picnic, in which material pleasure and human happiness blended very largely with spiritual experience."[6] There was an old saying that more souls were made than saved at camp meetings. I was one of those May–June camp-meeting babies.

Of course, this is why every teenager loves camp meetings. They are profoundly sensuous experiences, which is a source both of their power (for their defenders) and their peril (for their detractors).

Every tribe has a vibe. To pass on the tradition to the next generation is to imbibe and inscribe the vibe of the tribe until it becomes jive. This is what happens at camp meetings for holiness kids. At camp meetings we enjoyed God, battled Satan, and consecrated the commonplace. Most of all, I sensed the presence of God in the fragrance of nature's incense—the clean scent of the sawdust trail, the sweet odor of sap from the pine trees, the breath of smoke from fire altars and campfires. In Judaism, you knew God was present when you smelled the barbecue. In Catholicism, you knew God was present when you smelled the incense. In evangelical Protestantism, you knew God was present when you smelled the sawdust. There is an old camp meeting saying that when you get sawdust in your shoes, the sawdust gets in your soul, and you keep coming back. I remain convinced to this day that God likes the smell of sawdust.

Camp meetings were sometimes called "open-forest cathedrals" because they were held in nature's temple under the canopy of clouds by day and the chandelier of stars by night, when the night torches would cast their eerie shadows across the congregation in tents. They sensed the presence of God in touch: through the feeling of the earth for a mattress and splintery logs for a pew, through the touching of one another in forgiving embrace at the mourner's bench, in the kiss of peace at the "glory pen," and in the hand-clasping ceremony at the speaker's platform. Those in attendance sensed the presence of God in sound: with the voices singing, praying, and preaching. Evangelicals loved to pine after upcoming camp meetings, for they knew that "great shouters" would be there, as well as "plain preachers" who pioneered the use of anecdotes and illustrations. The poetry of camp meetings' spiritual ballads, praise hymns, and revival spirituals was not among the finest of American literature, but the emotionalized theology was straight from the heart of experience and was bold in expressing the freedom, joy, and forgiveness found in the Christian life.

There are some reports that preaching got so intense at camp meetings that people forgot to eat, but more often it was the case that God was sensed through taste. People looked forward to camp meetings for a month as a yearly oasis of hospitality in a desert of frontier loneliness and isolation—hospitality exhibited through sumptuous meals and cookouts. One report suggests that the August 1801 Cane Ridge camp meeting finally dispersed only because the twenty to thirty thousand attenders ran out of food.

Like any pilgrimage, camp meetings created a heightened sense of community and solidarity. The common involvement and camaraderie transcended all differences. When we went home, we fed off the stories and shared experiences for the year and regaled those who did not undertake the journey with new versions of God's "doings," which inspired and strengthened deeper religious commitment.

An ancient Jewish tradition was that a mother would weave a seamless garment for her son when he left home. This would have been soaked in spikenard. Both the seamless garment and the spikenard would be key features in the story of the Cross. Jesus was born smelling muck, and he died smelling muck. But out of life's mire and muck God can wrench and wring the musk of life's sweetest aromas. Out of the "offense" of the garbage dump called Golgotha (the Hebrew word for "offense" means "to smell bad") can God bring the best smells. Ambergris, highly prized by perfumers for its ability to capture and intensify fragrances, is actually whale excrement.[7]

I am still lighting matchboxes and smelling sawdust. Before I write a word I light candles, with my favorite fragrances either that of frankincense or the five spices that comprise incense, or the woody smells of the outdoors. The lit wax candles (I'm allergic to soy) and the smell of Notre Dame Cathedral help the ambience of writing and praying immensely.

I also agree to do at least one camp meeting every year, and I speak every three years at the longest continuous camp meeting in US history: the Taylor Tabernacle camp meeting outside Brownsville, Tennessee. I have agreed to speak at their two-hundred-year-anniversary camp in 2026.[8]

# 24

# LUMPS IN THE MATTRESS

---

*Shed your love in my heart, O God, until I can*
*see as You want me to see and feel as You want me*
*to feel and think as You want me to think.*

MABEL BOGGS SWEET

By now you know: I was raised in an evangelical petri dish. It was a home that let us roam on a long leash outdoors, but the reins were tightened indoors, regulating our daily schedules to redeem the time and restricting what we could watch on TV—even what we could read.

But read we did, under the cover of 1 Timothy 4:13 (KJV): "Give attendance to reading." We had little money, but there was always some for church and books. Mother would seldom walk by and ask, "What are you doing?" Instead we were asked, "What are you reading?" Mother treated great ideas as if they were people, and she wanted to get to know them better.

As I look back on a home where books lurked in every corner of every room, I can see how I have arrived now at a place of "bookishness," where the words "my life" and "my library" go together; to give up one is to give up the other. Home is where your books are. And every room has its own reading material: bathroom books, living room books, hallway books, bedroom books, dining room books, library books. One of the joys of my life is opening boxes of books, unpacking boxes of books, sending boxes of books. A delivery of books is my version of being handed a box of chocolates.

A book is more than a book. A book is a friend, a lover, a sparring partner, a vacation, a meal (some banquets, some snacks), a healer. Every book issues a "call." "Hearing the call" is another way of talking about reading, and answering the call is how you allow a book to change you.

In E. M. Forster's 1910 novel *Howards End*, a character comes to a glorious end when a column of books comes crashing down on him, smashing him to death. The only better way to die that I can think of is while preaching. Then there is Cornelius Jansen, the seventeenth-century bishop of Ypres (Belgium), who supposedly died from a disease contracted from the dust of old books. Writer and humorist Anita Renfro gave me some "Old Library" air freshener to spray in my study in case I'm not getting enough of the spores and smells of old books.

Our reading was closely scrutinized. No novels were allowed in the house—"not worth the candle" was Mother's dismissive castigation of the "frivolity of fiction." Novels were a way of "trifling" away one's time (a word she attributed to John Wesley). Novels were in a category of "useless literature," guilty of spinning "cobwebs of learning, admirable for the fineness of thread and work, but of no substance or profit."[1] So I took to sneaking into the house novels that I took out of the library, hiding them under the mattress. I would stash them under my sneakers in my gym bag. From trial and error I figured out how many I could hide under the mattress without lumps. Since my brothers and I changed the sheets, the reasoning went, Mother wouldn't look there if there were no lumps in the mattress.

Every time I did pull a novel out, I admit, I felt a bit guilty—a guilt trip Mother is still tour-guiding from her grave whenever I pick up a novel, even those written by Christian novelists like Marilynne Robinson, Dorothy Sayers, Lisa Samson, J. R. R. Tolkien, or those we used to refer to as "Catholic novelists" like Graham Greene, Muriel Spark, Evelyn Waugh, and Francois Mauriac. The guilt was my hardest hurdle when I first tried my hand at fiction. The whole time I was working with my colleague and coauthor Lori Wagner on *The Seraph Seal*,[2] I was haunted by the question *Is this too much superficiality and too little sinew?* But once I enter the story of any novelist, I am always grateful for how literature enables us to live more lives and more eras than our own.

We knew which authors Mother liked and which she didn't. She liked Uncle Buddy Robinson, whose *Sweet*

*Honey in the Rock* was a favorite. She didn't like the evangelist John R. Rice, whose 1941 book *Bobbed Hair, Bossy Wives, and Women Preachers* was on the forbidden list. We never saw a copy, but we knew almost everything in it. It seemed as if we had in our little house everything John Wesley and John Bunyan and John Fletcher wrote.

I thought growing up that Susanna Wesley must have written a handbook on child rearing because Mother referenced her so much. She was Mother's hero and role model. In fact, Mother raised us in the company of women: Deborah ("If the Lord couldn't find a man, he used a woman"), Rahab (we didn't learn she was a prostitute until our teens), Miriam, Lydia, Junia (Mother's "mystery woman"), Madame Guyon (surely a biblical writer, I thought—Mother quoted her so much), Anne Morrow Lindbergh, Madame Chiang Kai-Shek, and Phoebe.

Who was Phoebe? I was never sure. Sometimes her name seemed to be linked with Paul and the book of Romans. Mother's suspicion that Phoebe was more than Paul's "helper"[3] has been proven right by biblical scholars who have argued that *prostasis* means "president," "superintendent," or someone "set over others." If only Mother had known the *Centenary Translation* (1924) of Helen Barrett Montgomery, the first woman to have a professional company publish her English translation of the Greek New Testament and the first woman to head up a denomination in the United States (Northern Baptist Convention, 1921). Montgomery's translation of the *hapax legomenon prostasis* goes like this:

I commend to you our sister Phoebe, who is a
minister of the church at Cenchrea.

I beg you to give her a Christian welcome, as
the saints should; and to assist her in any matter in
which she may have need of you. For she herself has
been made an overseer to many people, including
myself.[4]

But at other times Phoebe was a fuzzy figure who wrote
books and hymns and talked about the "latter rain" and
"concerts of prayer" and whose metaphor of "the altar" was
the centering fact of our existence. Only in college would I
learn that this second Phoebe was Phoebe Palmer, the most
important woman theologian in the Protestant experience
before our time.[5]

When W. W. Norton published my PhD thesis without
my having to change its dissertation diapers, Mother was
unimpressed. "It's not worthy of you to brag about something
like that, or to write a book just to advance your academic
career." In Mother's mind you wore any learning lightly, and
you wrote a book only to advance Christ and promote understanding of him so that, as Paul put it, "we will no longer be
immature like children . . . tossed and blown about by every
wind of new teaching."[6] Mother would subject books to a
smell test: Any hint that the book was written not to inform
or form the reader into the image of Christ but to impress
the reader and promote or protect the writer, and she would
sniff her nose at it and refuse to read it.

There was no choice involved in whether or not my brothers and I would get an education. The assumption was that we would all get graduate degrees, and we would all get scholarships that would pay for it. Our only "choice" was what we would be educated in. For parents on the edge of penury and without college degrees, to have all three of their children receive PhD degrees is a testimony to Mother's resolution and will.

At the same time, when we were old enough to understand the nuance, Mother was insistent that no one can "teach" anyone anything. We can only teach ourselves under the "anointing" of the Spirit: "I do not write to you because you do not know the truth, but because you do know it. . . . You do not need anyone to teach you. But as his anointing teaches you about all things."[7]

The teacher you can trust is the one who insists, "Don't take it from me," who insists that you listen to those disclosures that come from within. Your inner voice is the ultimate teacher, which Mother insisted is the voice of the Holy Spirit, the only one you should "take it from." To this day I tell my students, "If I'm not saying something that you haven't thought all along, or felt but didn't have words for, or that doesn't resonate deeply in your soul, then don't take it from me." Insight is truly the sight that comes from *inside* you, not outside of you. All true learning is from inside out, not outside in.[8]

But the outside voice is what makes your inside voice real and alive. You need the outside voice to activate your inside voice and to allow you to trust it.

In Matthew's Gospel, the favored conception of Jesus is as Teacher and of the disciples as students or learners. In all our learning, teachers impressed on us the contrast between the malleability of all religious teachings and the reliability of Jesus. The Great Commission ("Therefore go and make disciples of all nations"[9]) means to enroll people in the Jesus School. *Disciple* (*mathetes*) means "learner"; it is Matthew's favorite word for a follower of Jesus. No one can be a "teacher" of the truth of Jesus Christ. There is only one Teacher. We are all *mathetes*. We are at all times learners, never learned.[10]

The same is true for the church. A teaching church that isn't a learning church is an unlearning church, an untutored church, and hence an ignorant church, disguised and protected by the teaching function of the church. Teaching comes with huge responsibilities: "You're hopeless, you religion scholars! You took the key of knowledge, but instead of unlocking doors, you locked them. You won't go in yourself, and won't let anyone else in either."[11] The second-worst thing any of Mother's boys could do would be to enter the ivory tower and then close the doors or lock them behind us, keeping knowledge to ourselves.

But the very worst thing any of us could have done would have been to leave Jesus behind in our learning. Paul's metaphor of "a resounding gong or a clanging symbol"[12] wasn't just a metaphor. At the back of Greek amphitheaters were thirteen tuned bronze vases, neatly arranged as loudspeakers would be today. They would pick up the sound of the actor's voice and amplify it. Without love, Paul is saying, we are as empty as the acoustic amplifiers of the Greek theaters, which were full of sound but empty of any meaning or truth (the plays were total decadence). In his sermon connecting scholarship and the Song of Songs, St. Bernard wrote,

> And should any of you desire to attain to an understanding of the things which he reads, let him love. For it is useless of him who loves not, to attempt to read or listen to this Canticle of love, because the "ignited" word can obtain no lodgment in a heart that is cold and frozen.[13]

In the 1960s there was a television program called *Hogan's Heroes*. One of the characters, Sergeant Schultz, had a signature line: "I know nothing." It's actually an echo of Socrates, one of the wisest of philosophers, who liked to say, "To know is to know that you know nothing. That is the meaning of true knowledge." Mother loved that line, "I know nothing." In fact, Mother was "determined," as she put it, to be like Paul: "to know nothing . . . except Jesus Christ and him crucified."[14] Of course, by saying that, she was proudly announcing that she knew everything—at least everything important there was to know. Jesus is not an opinion. Jesus is not one option among many. Jesus is the Way, the Truth, and the Life. If he wants our opinion, he'll give it to us.

Two hundred years ago, German poet Heinrich Heine

(1797–1856) stood before Our Lady of Amiens Cathedral, the tallest cathedral in France, and lamented the loss of "convictions" that build cathedrals. In a world that has suburbanized the stars, his words hurt the ears, like a Jack Nicholson "you-can't-handle-the-truth" moment.

> This work is a Gothic cathedral, whose columns rising to heaven, and whose colossal dome, seem to have been raised by the bold hand of a giant; while the innumerable daintily fine festoons, rosettes, and arabesques which are spread over it, like a veil of lace in stone, testify to the unwearied patience of dwarfs. A giant in the conception and forming of the whole, a dwarf in the laborious execution of details, the architect of the Huguenots is as far beyond our intelligence as the composers of the old cathedrals. When I lately stood with a friend before that of Amiens, and he beheld with awe and pity that monument of giant strength in towering stone, and of dwarfish patience in minute sculpture, he asked me how it happens that we can no longer build such piles? I replied, "Dear Alphonse, men in those days had convictions; we moderns have opinions, and it requires something more than an opinion to build such a Gothic cathedral."[15]

Or, as Mother used to sing it as a lullaby out of one of the songbooks she kept on the old upright piano:

*We are building every day,*
*In a good or evil way;*
*Till in every arch and line,*
*All our faults and failings shine;*

*And the structure, as it grows,*
*Will our inmost self disclose.*
*It may grow a castle grand,*
*Or a wreck upon the sand.*

*Do you ask what building this,*
*That can show both pain and bliss,*
*That can be both dark and fair?*
*Lo! Its name is Character.*

*Build it well, whate'er you do;*
*Build it straight and strong and true;*
*Build it clean and high and broad:*
*Build it for the eye of God.*

Mother had built her cathedral in each one of us.

*Conclusion*

# THE KITE

———— ❦ ————

*I have not always been where I am today. But I have*
*come a long ways and I hope in the tomorrows I can*
*keep on saying there is still more ground to possess.*

MABEL BOGGS SWEET,
REFLECTING ON JAMES 1:4

Mother taught us to judge ourselves in a large way. If
you are hunting deer in dragon country, you must
keep your eye peeled for dragons. But when you are hunting
dragons, you can ignore the deer.

We were bred to be dragonflies. My mother tongue
was the language of a metamorphic faith. The crisis of the
chrysalis church is its inability to fly or to unfold wings for
a takeoff.

One of our favorite trips was to the raging waters of
Niagara Falls. But I was always less interested in the falls
themselves than in the suspension bridge that went over the

falls and in Mother's story of a little boy named Homan J. Walsh and his little kite that helped build the first bridge.

When Homan J. Walsh died in Lincoln, Nebraska, on 8 March 1899, local newspapers noted that he had been a thirty-year resident of the city, a real estate businessman, officer of the Lincoln Gas Company, and a past city council member. Of greater interest to Nebraskans, both then and now, however, was Walsh's unique boyhood contribution to the suspension bridge over the Niagara River. In the fall of 1847, civil engineer Charles Ellet Jr. of Philadelphia was commissioned to construct a bridge at the narrowest point of Niagara Gorge, immediately above the whirlpool rapids. Ellet was about to begin when he faced his first obstacle.

The building of a suspension bridge is begun with the stretching of a line or wire across the stream. However, the turbulent rapids, the eight-hundred-foot-wide gap, and the 225-foot-high cliffs of the whirlpool gorge made a direct crossing impossible.

It occurred to someone that a kite might be a way to bridge the chasm. Accordingly, a cash prize was offered to the first boy who could fly his kite, with a line attached, to the opposite bank. There was a tremendous turnout of American and Canadian boys for a contest held in January 1848. The first to succeed in spanning the gorge with his kite, named the *Union*, was Homan J. Walsh.

In order to take advantage of more favorable winds, Walsh had crossed to the Canadian side of the gorge by ferry just below Niagara Falls and walked the two miles along the top of the cliff to the bridge site. At midnight, when a lull in the wind occurred, he flew his kite high above the gorge, and it reached the American side. But there was a sudden pull of the line, and it went limp. It had broken. To make matters worse, Walsh found himself marooned in Canada for eight days because river ice prevented the ferry from operating.

Finally Walsh was able to cross to the American side of the river and retrieve his kite. He then returned to the Canadian side, where he again flew the kite to the opposite bank. The kite string was fastened to a tree on the American shoreline, and a cord attached to it was pulled across. This time it didn't break.

After the kite and the cord came a heavier cord. Then a rope. Finally a wire cable, which was the beginning of the new bridge that was completed on 26 July 1848.

The bridge over which have crossed millions of people and monster machines all began with one small kite. The longest journeys start by taking the smallest steps. God took the first step and sent Jesus to cross over to our side, becoming the bridge, the Way, across the chasms of life.

Every day of her life, Mother hoisted aloft her kite of faith. She taught me the romance of flying. She taught me to resist the desire to control flight—to stick pins in a butterfly as soon as it flies and to frame it on the wall.

She also taught me, in her life and words, that if your mission can be completed in your lifetime, it isn't a big enough dream.

# NOTES

## INTRODUCTION

1. Mother's "southern" funeral service was conducted at the Covington Wesleyan Church, a church she helped plant. James Barnhart officiated at her funeral.

2. Walter Benjamin, *The Arcades Project*, trans. Howard Eiland and Kevin McLaughlin (Cambridge, MA: Belknap Press, 1999), 461.

3. Vladimir Nabokov, *Transparent Things* (New York: McGraw-Hill, 1972).

4. See Clare Griffiths, "The Patron Saint of Patrons," *The Times Literary Supplement*, June 27, 2014, 17.

5. See Luke 2:19 for an example of pondering.

6. Luke 2:51.

7. With thanks to Jean Fleming for this metaphor.

8. Steven Ozment's *The Serpent and The Lamb: Cranach, Luther, and the Making of the Reformation* (New Haven, CT: Yale University Press, 2012) portrays Cranach as key to Luther's resistance to the iconoclasm of some of his more zealous colleagues. "Cranach's various portraits of Luther, endlessly reproduced as prints, burnished his reputation for piety and discredited Catholic pictures of him as (for instance) a 'false prophet with seven heads.' This marketing campaign arguably made Luther's face the most famous in Europe. Cranach's illustrations for Luther's German Bible aided its prodigious commercial success."

9. For an initial exploring of this, see the chapter "Open Yourself to God's Story" in Leonard Sweet, *What Matters Most* (Colorado Springs: Waterbrook, 2004).

10. Philippians 3:8, NAB.

11. 2 Timothy 4:13.

12. Philippians 3:10, NAB.

13. Walt Whitman, *Leaves of Grass* (New York: Bantam Classic, 1983), 292.

14. See the introductory essay "The Things That Matter," in Sherry Turkle, ed., *Evocative Objects: Things We Think With* (Cambridge, MA: MIT Press, 2007), 3–10.

15. Amy Bloom, *Lucky Us* (New York: Penguin Random House, 2014), 186.

16. Turkle, ed., *Evocative Objects*, 5.

17. Daniel Miller, *Stuff* (London: Polity Press, 2009).

18. Ephesians 5:23, NKJV.

19. Václav Cílek, *To Breathe with Birds*, trans. Evan W. Mellander (Philadelphia: University of Pennsylvania Press, 2015), 83.

20. Claude Lévi-Strauss, *The Savage Mind* (Chicago: University of Chicago Press, 1961).

21. "The notion of 'mindless' materiality is a confusion." Rowan Williams, *The Edge of Words* (London: Bloomsbury, 2014), 147.
22. Sylvia Plath, "Black Rook in Rainy Weather," in *The Collected Poems*, ed. Ted Hughes (New York: Harper Perennial, 1981), 56.
23. Antonio Gramsci, "The Study of Philosophy," in *Cultural Resistance: A Reader*, ed. Stephen Duncombe (London: Verso, 2002), 60.
24. This is the argument of the French philosopher Gaston Bachelard (1884–1962), in words that comfort all collectors.
25. In late medieval Christianity, "the dominant scientific opinion was that an object of vision emits rays, which enter the onlooker's eyes with all the dangers and powers this contact entails." Bettina Bildhauer, "Ladies who Look," *Times Literary Supplement*, 2 July 2014, 22.

## CHAPTER 1: MA'S WEDDING RING, DAD'S HELLEVISION

1. Visit the website of Mother's church plant at www.asburywesleyan.com.
2. 2 Corinthians 6:14, KJV.
3. For the importance of being "released," see Phoebe Palmer, "Did the Lord Release You?", in *The Guide to Holiness, and Class-Leader's Magazine*, ed. John Bate (London: Amos Osborne, 1871), 271–273.
4. See Ian Bradley, *The Call to Seriousness* (New York: Lion, 2006), 29.
5. Mother's journal entry, 22 February 1957.
6. See F. Scott Fitzgerald's "Bernice Bobs Her Hair," in *Bernice Bobs Her Hair and Other Stories* (New York: Signet Classic, 1996).
7. Psalm 31:8, MT.
8. Acts 18:10.
9. Maxine L. Haines and Lee M. Haines, *Celebrate Our Daughters: 150 Years of Women in Wesleyan Ministry* (Fishers, IN: Wesleyan Publishing House, 2004).

## CHAPTER 2: THE YELLOW-PAINTED POT-METAL BOUDOIR LIGHT

1. "Shamgar Had an Oxgoad, David Had a Sling," in *Ruth Overholtzer*, comp., *Salvation Songs for Children* 4 (Warrenton, MO: International Child Evangelism Fellowship, 1951).
2. F. E. Belden, "Building Every Day (Motion Song)," in W. B. Olmstead and T. Harris, eds., *Light and Life Songs* (Chicago: W. B. Rose, 1904), 147.
3. "There Were Twelve Disciples," accessed September 8, 2016, at http://www.hymnary .org/text/there_were_twelve_disciples_jesus_called.
4. 1 Samuel 14:43; Joshua 7:21; Exodus 17:12; 2 Samuel 5:22-25; 1 Samuel 30:7; 1 Samuel 6:1-5; 2 Samuel 24:21-25; 2 Samuel 6:11.

## CHAPTER 3: ROCKS

1. George Herbert, "Man," in *The Works of George Herbert*, ed. F. E. Hutchison (Oxford: Clarendon Press, 1941), 91.
2. George Lemuel Boggs, born 2 May 1884, died 15 January 1973. Ida Blanch McCarty, born 25 October 1890, died 22 March 1966. My grandparents were married on 26 December 1906 at the home of her parents, R. Frank McCarty (Pocohontas Co., WV) and Eliza Jane Alderman McCarty (Greenbriar Co., WV). Rev. George Beets presided. GL was the son of George J. Boggs and Mary Ellen Pyles Boggs.
3. Jonathan Edwards, "Of Being (1721)," in *A Jonathan Edwards Reader*, ed. John E. Smith, Harry S. Stout, and Kenneth P. Minkema (New Haven, CT: Yale University Press, 1995), 13.

4. 2 Chronicles 6:18.
5. "And I, even I only, am left; and they seek my life, to take it away." 1 Kings 19:10, 14, KJV.
6. Exodus 19:12.
7. Deuteronomy 32:13; Psalm 81:16.
8. Terry Eagleton, *Reason, Faith, and Revolution: Reflections on the God Debate* (New Haven, CT: Yale University Press, 2009), 8-9.
9. Matthew 28:20, KJV.
10. Psalm 19:1-2, NKJV.
11. Romans 8:22.
12. Isaiah 11:6, KJV.
13. Ephesians 1:8-12; cf. Colossians 1:20.
14. Galatians 3:27-28. See also Leonard Sweet, *Me and We: God's New Social Gospel* (Nashville: Abingdon Press, 2014).

## CHAPTER 4: THE DREADED FOUR-WAY

1. 1 John 2:21.
2. Luke 4:13.

## CHAPTER 5: THE FAMILY BIBLE AT FAMILY PRAYER

1. In the language of Sherry Turkle's book *Evocative Objects: Things We Think With* (Cambridge, MA: MIT Press, 2007).
2. Song of Solomon 1:6, ESV.
3. See Ezekiel 3:1.
4. 1 Corinthians 9:10.
5. See John 6:63.
6. Richard Burgin, "Isaac Bashevis Singer's Universe," *New York Times Magazine*, December 3, 1978, 40.
7. See Psalm 119:11.
8. Peter Ochs, "Morning Prayer as Redemptive Thinking," in *Liturgy, Time, and the Politics of Redemption*, ed. Randi Rashkover and C. C. Pecknold (Grand Rapids, MI: Eerdmans, 2006), 50–90.
9. Romans 10:17.
10. Galatians 3:2.
11. Psalm 1:3.
12. The *Times Literary Supplement* held a symposium in 1977 asking poets and philosophers to choose and comment on the most overrated and underrated books of the twentieth century.
13. See 1 John 2:7-8: "Dear friends, I am not writing you a new command but an old one, which you have had since the beginning. This old command is the message you have heard. Yet I am writing you a new command; its truth is seen in him and in you."
14. The Church of England, *A Catechism*, accessed September 15, 2016 at https://www.church ofengland.org/prayer-worship/worship/book-of-common-prayer/a-catechism.aspx.
15. Barth argued against bibliolatry most forcefully in *Church Dogmatics* I.1 (London: T & T Clark, 1975), 125–126.

## CHAPTER 6: UPRIGHT PIANO AND SOUNDTRACK FOR THE SOUL

1. Colossians 3:16.

2. For Garrison Keillor on playing bassoon as a high school student, see http://prairiehome
   .publicradio.org/programs/20030419/bassoon.shtml.
3. Marion Jacobson, *Squeeze This! A Cultural History of the Accordion in America*
   (Springfield, IL: University of Illinois Press, 2012).
4. Matthew 26:30.
5. Philip Bliss, "Wonderful Words of Life" (1874).
6. Ibid.
7. F. F. Bruce, *The Epistle of Paul to the Romans*, Tyndale New Testament Commentaries
   (Grand Rapids, MI: Eerdmans, 1963).
8. Colossians 3:16, DRV.
9. The hope for the future of classical music is in the East. For example, the Sichuan
   Conservatory in Chengdu is said to have more than 10,000 students (the Juilliard in
   New York has eight hundred), and low-end estimates of the number of Chinese children
   learning piano is 30 million.

## CHAPTER 7: POLIO BRACES

1. In graduate school I discovered these exact same words in the writings of Flannery
   O'Connor (1925–1964): "I think that the Church is the only thing that is going to make
   the terrible world we are coming to endurable; the only thing that makes the Church
   endurable is that it is somehow the body of Christ and that on this we are fed. It seems
   to be a fact that you have to suffer as much from the Church as for it but if you believe
   in the divinity of Christ, you have to cherish the world at the same time that you struggle
   to endure it" (*Flannery O'Connor: Collected Works*, ed. Sally Fitzgerald, p. 942). I'm sure
   Mother never read Flannery O'Connor, but she did have a magpie mind. Or maybe she
   came up with the same words to describe the same experiences she shared with O'Connor.
2. Neal Ascherson, "Lust for Leaks," *London Review of Books*, September 1, 2005, http://
   www.lrb.co.uk/v27/n17/neal-ascherson/lust-for-leaks.
3. Luke 24:11, KJV.
4. Acts 9:5, KJV.
5. Attributed to Leopold Godowsky in Carol Tavris, "Termites and Penguins," *Times
   Literary Supplement*, January 7, 2011, 23.
6. See 1 Peter 4:12.

## CHAPTER 8: YELLOW CHEESE

1. James Baldwin, *Collected Essays* (New York: Library of America, 1998), 173.
2. William Blake, "With Happiness Stretch'd across the Hills," in *Letters from William Blake
   to Thomas Butts, 1800–1803*, printed in facsimile with an introductory note by Geoffrey
   Keynes (Oxford: Clarendon Press, 1926).
3. Matthew 25:35, NLT.
4. Gerard W. Hughes, *Cry of Wonder* (New York: Bloomsbury Continuum, 2014), 181.
5. See Romans 1:18-25.
6. Tennessee Williams, *Sweet Bird of Youth: Acting Edition* (New York: Dramatists Play
   Service, 1962), 31.

## CHAPTER 9: SWEET'S LINIMENT

1. Waterman Sweet, *Views of Anatomy; and Practice of Bonesetting by a Mechanical Process
   Different from All Book Knowledge* (Schenectady, NY: Riggs, 1844).

2. The announcement of M&B 693 (the first chemical treatment for pneumonia) was revolutionary. Sulfonamide drugs, launched in the mid-1930s, represented the first medicinal treatment for a whole range of bacterial diseases. The German company I. G. Farben introduced a drug called Prontosil in 1935, and researchers in Britain and the United States made further advances in the ensuing decade. By the 1940s, they had developed antibiotics that offered better results, fewer side effects, and more versatile applications than their sulfonamide predecessors.

3. "Stephen Sweet's Infallible Linament [*sic*] Bottle," Odyssey's Virtual Museum, accessed September 19, 2016, http://odysseysvirtualmuseum.com/products/StephenSweet'sInfallible LinamentBottle.html.

4. Proverbs 23:7, KJV.

5. For more, see my book *Health and Medicine in the Evangelical Tradition* (Norcross, GA: Trinity Press International, 1994).

6. See Isaiah 45:22.

7. Jerome, *Lives of Illustrious Men*, trans. Ernest Cushing Richardson, PhD (London: Aeterna, 2016).

8. Eusebius, sermon on St. Luke. See Gordon Franz, "Luke the Physician: With Medicine for the Souls," accessed September 30, 2016, http://www.biblearchaeology.org/post/2014 /01/23/Luke-The-Physician-with-Medicine-for-the-Souls.aspx#Article. These sermons by Eusebius and Jerome inspired me to write *The Jesus Prescription for a Healthy Life* (Nashville: Abingdon Press, 1996).

9. Charles Wesley, "Father, Whose Everlasting Love," 1741.

10. Robert G. Tuttle, Jr., "John Wesley and the Gifts of the Holy Spirit," The Unofficial Confessing Movement, accessed September 19, 2016, http://www.ucmpage.org/articles /rtuttle1.html.

## CHAPTER 10: LYE SOAP

1. 2 Corinthians 12:14-15, KJV.

2. Romans 12:1, KJV.

3. Romans 5:3-4.

4. Matthew 12:36, NASB.

## CHAPTER 11: MOUNDS, MARS BARS, AND THE COUNTY HOME

1. Richard Foster, *Streams of Living Water* (San Francisco: HarperOne, 1998).

2. See Vatican II's "Declaration on the Relation of the Church to Non-Christian Religions" (*Nostra Aetate*), para. 2, accessed September 19, 2016, at http://www.vatican.va/archive /hist_councils/ii_vatican_council/documents/vat-ii_decl_19651028_nostra-aetate _en.html.

3. Thomas Aquinas *Summa Theologiae* 1a47.1, accessed September 19, 2016, at http:// dhspriory.org/thomas/summa/FP/FP047.html#FPQ47OUTP1.

## CHAPTER 12: THE MYSTERY BAG AND THE CURIOSITY CABINET

1. Psalm 34:8.

2. John 20:28.

3. Matthew 22:46.

4. Revelation 15:8.

5. Augustine, *Epistula* 11.14.

6. 2 Peter 2:12.

7. Lamentations 1:12.

8. Marc Allum, *The Collector's Cabinet: Tales, Facts and Fictions from the World of Antiques* (London: Icon, 2015), 92.

9. Nehemiah 8:10.

10. See Matthew 27:19-26.

11. Jessica L. Malay, *The Case of Mistress Mary Hampson: Her Story of Marital Abuse and Defiance in Seventeenth-Century England* (Stanford, CA: Stanford University Press, 2014).

12. 1 Corinthians 13:4, KJV, adapted.

## CHAPTER 13: EXTRA PLATE AT THE TABLE

1. So says Henry Shapiro in his book *Appalachia on Our Mind* (Chapel Hill, NC: University of North Carolina Press, 1986).

2. Loretta Lynn, quoted in "Who Talks Funny?", *Kentucky New Era*, January 24, 1977.

3. Adrienne Rich, "Readings of History," in *Snapshots of a Daughter-in-Law* (New York: W. W. Norton, 1967), 39.

4. Langston Hughes, "Mother to Son," (1923), accessed September 19, 2016, at http://www.poemhunter.com/poem/mother-to-son.

5. See Luke 22:7-23.

6. 1 Corinthians 10:21.

7. Leo Tolstoy, *Anna Karenina*, (New York: Random House, 2000), 3.

8. John 4:24.

9. Psalm 23:5.

10. For more on this, see my book *From Tablet to Table* (Colorado Springs: NavPress, 2015).

11. Peter Ochs, *Peirce, Pragmatism, and the Logic of Scripture* (Cambridge: Cambridge University Press, 1998), 319. Emphasis in original.

## CHAPTER 14: DAD'S ROLLTOP DESK AND HIS SECRET COMPARTMENT

1. *Do You Want to Be an Actor?* with Haven MacQuarrie was broadcast from January 3 until May 2, 1937, a series that continued on Sundays at 10:30 p.m. as a half-hour show from December 5, 1937, until February 20, 1938.

2. George Barna calls these "SSI," or strategic sources of influence. By the way, the church either doesn't appear on the list or is way, way down the list. See an interview with George Barna at http://www.homileticsonline.com/subscriber/interviews/barna.asp.

3. Pablo Picasso, *Picasso on Art: A Selection of Views*, ed. Dore Ashton (New York: Viking Press, 1972), 21.

4. See "Letters to the Editor: Michael Servetus," *Times Literary Supplement,* January 4, 2013, http://www.the-tls.co.uk/articles/private/michael-servetus/.

5. Romans 7:14-16, NKJV.

6. Immanuel Kant, quoted in *G. E. Moore: Early Philosophical Writings*, ed. Thomas Baldwin and Consuelo Preti (Cambridge: Cambridge University Press, 2011), 206.

7. Matthew 28:15, WEB.

8. 1 John 3:2, RSV.

9. Romans 8:21, NKJV.

10. John 8:36.

11. Although Mother was unyieldingly a teetotaler in front of us, in her notebooks (reflecting on 1 Peter 4:3-4) she did admit that wine itself was not forbidden. "It was an excess of wine that was the problem."

12. Romans 14:14; 1 Corinthians 3:21-22.

## CHAPTER 15: GRAMMA'S GREEN PORCELAIN WOOD STOVE

1. This story is told by Vietnamese Buddhist scholar and teacher Thich Nhat Hanh in an interview with Diane Wolkstein, "Beyond Views: An Exchange with Thich Nhat Hanh," *Parabola*, Winter 2005, 21.

2. Deuteronomy 30:20, NKJV.

3. Deuteronomy 31:6, GNT.

4. Deuteronomy 31:8, MSG.

5. Denise Levertov, "Death Psalm: O Lord of Mysteries," in *Poems 1972–1982* (New York: New Directions, 2001), 108–109.

6. Betsy Barron, quoted by Joanna Adams, "A Matter of Time," July 28, 2002, accessed September 21, 2016, at http://fourthchurch.org/sermons/2002/072802.html.

## CHAPTER 16: THE DOCTOR'S SCRIPT

1. Gayle Carlton Felton, "John Wesley and the Teaching Ministry," in *Journal of Religious Education* 92, no. 1 (1997), 96.

2. John Milton, *Areopagitica; A Speech of Mr. John Milton for the Liberty of Unlicenc'd Printing, to the Parliament of England* (1644), accessed September 21, 2016, http://www.columbia.edu/itc/journalism/j6075/edit/readings/areopagitica_milton.html.

3. 1 John 3:1; Galatians 3:27; Luke 17:21; 1 John 4:13; Colossians 1:27; Ephesians 4:22-24.

4. Luke 16:1-13.

5. Leonard Sweet, *Soul Salsa* (Grand Rapids, MI: Zondervan, 2000). In the same interview I was attacked for the "blasphemy" of the title, and for associating Jesus with dancing. When I replied that I actually got the comparison of faith to a dance from Jesus (Matthew 11:17), the interviewers challenged me with "Then why did you pick such a sensual dance?" I asked them what better dance to pick? One of them replied with no hesitation, "What's wrong with a square dance?" I didn't bother to say the obvious: A book entitled *Soul Square Dance* might not pack much punch.

6. Thomas Aquinas, quoted in *Covenant-Making: The Fabric of Relationship*, ed. Charles Conniry and Laura Simmons (Eugene, OR: Pickwick, 2014), 175.

7. 1 John 2:15.

8. John 3:16.

9. See Matthew 10:16.

## CHAPTER 17: NAUTICAL DOOR

1. Mother loved the story of Hannah, mother of Samuel, and loved the verse "For this child I prayed; and the LORD hath given me my petition which I asked of him" (1 Samuel 1:27, KJV).

2. Matthew 6:6, GNT.

3. See Luke 14:18.

4. Dante Aligheri, *Dante's Inferno in Plain and Simple English* (CreateSpace, 2012), canto 1.

5. See Isaiah 47:10.

6. Isaiah 57:15; Psalm 18:35.

7. "Do nothing out of selfish ambition or vain conceit. Rather, in humility value others

above yourselves, not looking to your own interests, but each of you to the interests of the others" (Philippians 2:3-4).

8. Blaise Pascal, *Pensées*, trans. W. F. Trotter (Mineola, NY: Dover, 2003), 121.

9. Josemaría Escrivá, *The Way* (New York: Doubleday, 2006), 57.

10. 1 Corinthians 8:1.

11. Philippians 4:13; John 15:5, NKJV.

## CHAPTER 18: GRANDFATHER'S CHAIR

1. As best I can tell, his dates are 8 November 1877–4 June 1942, although that would have meant that my father was born when he was thirty-seven years of age.

2. Genesis 3:21, MSG.

3. Ira Sweet was a frequent delegate to the Susquehanna Annual Conference. For example, in the minutes of the session held in Rome, New York, on 20–25 September 1905, with Bishop Wilson T. Hogue presiding, twenty-eight-year-old Ira Sweet is listed as the delegate from the Gloversville/Johnstown Circuit.

## CHAPTER 19: GLOVER'S MANGE CURE

1. Joshua 24:15.

2. 2 Thessalonians 3:11.

3. John 9:4, MT.

4. Guy Elmes, quoted in Kristen Hohenadel, "Shooting for an 'Affair' They'll Remember," *Los Angeles Times*, December 24, 1999, http://articles.latimes.com/1999/dec/24/entertainment/ca-46957.

5. John Richardson, "Picasso and Gertrude Stein: Mano a Mano, Tete-a-Tete," *New York Times*, 10 February 1991, accessed September 30, 2016, at http://www.nytimes.com/1991/02/10/arts/art-picasso-and-gertrude-stein-mano-a-mano-tete-a-tete.html?pagewanted=all.

6. Samuel Johnson, *The Letters of Samuel Johnson, Volume II: 1773–1776*, ed. Bruce Redford (Princeton, NJ: Princeton University Press, 1992), 313.

7. From the Elizabeth Clephane hymn "Beneath the Cross of Jesus" (1868), accessed September 22, 2016, at http://www.hymnary.org/text/beneath_the_cross_of_jesus_i_fain_would.

8. 1 Corinthians 6:19-20.

## CHAPTER 21: CHOCOLATE ÉCLAIRS

1. John 5:17.

2. Bertolt Brecht, "Justice Is the Bread of the People," in *Bertolt Brecht: Poems 1913–1956* (London: Methuen, 1980).

3. "In my opinion this child don't need to have his head shrunk at all. Juvenile delinquency is purely a social disease!" "Gee, Officer Krupke," *West Side Story* (1961), lyrics accessed September 22, 2016, at http://www.westsidestory.com/site/level2/lyrics/krupke.html.

4. *Waiting for Godot*, quoted in David S. Cunningham, "Do Not Presume," *Christian Century*, 23 March 2010, accessed September 30, 2016, at http://christiancentury.org/article/2010-03/do-not-presume.

## CHAPTER 22: THE WRINGER

1. Luther is credited with the phrase "God himself has died" by Georg Hegel in *The Phenomenology of Mind*, trans. J. B. Baillie (Mineola, NY: Dover, 2003).

## CHAPTER 23: MATCHBOXES AND SAWDUST

1. In the words of the old proverb, "We will bear with the stink, if it bring but in chink."
2. Whenever I bring Nexus Therappe shampoo to a lather on my head, I bathe my being in memories of wonderful times with my oldest son at Newcomb Hollow Beach near South Wellfleet, Cape Cod. I used to use a coconut-scented suntan oil to protect his baby skin.
3. In talking with others about their favorite smells, I have discovered regional differences. East Coast people prefer floral scents, and Northerners the smell of the seasons. Southerners seem to prefer hearty snorts of pine. Midwesterners like the whiff of hay and farm animals. Westerners like the aroma of barbecuing meat. I like them all.
4. "The new inhabitant . . . has no conception of the oyster-like tenacity with which an old settler . . . clings to the spot where his successive generations have been embedded." Nathaniel Hawthorne, *The Scarlet Letter* (South Kingstown, MD: Millennium, 2015), 8.
5. Francis Asbury, *Swallowed Up in God* (CreateSpace, 2014), 62.
6. Mary Clemmer Ames, *Eirene: Or, A Woman's Right* (New York: Putnam and Sons, 1872), 68.
7. The sperm whale vacuums up three hundred to seven hundred squid a day. It has the largest brain of any mammal, three times the weight of our own. The twenty-foot head of the sperm whale was valued for the oil (spermaceti) that it contained: a fuel that didn't freeze for street lights and a lubricant for the mechanisms of watches.
8. By then I hope to have finished my story of the two thousand continuous camp meetings still in existence; I am titling it *Beulah Land*.

## CHAPTER 24: LUMPS IN THE MATTRESS

1. Francis Bacon, "Empiricism," from *Francis Bacon: The Major Works*, ed. Brian Vickers (Oxford: Oxford University Press, 2002), 140.
2. Leonard Sweet and Lori Wagner, *The Seraph Seal* (Nashville: Thomas Nelson, 2011).
3. Romans 16:1-2, NKJV.
4. Romans 16:2, *Centenary Translation*. See also J. Alfred Smith Sr., *The African-American Pulpit*, Spring 2010, 55–56.
5. See Thomas Oden's *Phoebe Palmer: Selected Writings*, Classics of Western Spirituality (Mahwah, NJ: Paulist Press, 1988).
6. Ephesians 4:14, NLT.
7. 1 John 2:21, 27.
8. See a similar affirmation by Steve Jobs in his now-famous commencement address at Stanford: "Your time is limited, so don't waste it. . . . Don't be trapped by dogma. . . . Don't let the noise of others' opinions drown out your inner voice. And most important, have the courage to follow your heart and intuition. They somehow already know what you truly want to become. Everything else is secondary." Accessed September 22, 2016, at http://news.stanford.edu/2005/06/14/jobs-061505/.
9. Matthew 28:19.
10. See chapter 5 in Leonard Sweet, *Summoned to Lead* (Grand Rapids, MI: Zondervan, 2004).
11. Luke 11:52, MSG.
12. 1 Corinthians 13:1.
13. St. Bernard, "The Bond of Love by Which the Bride Holds the Bridegroom and Will Not Let Him Go," Sermon 79 on the Song of Songs.
14. 1 Corinthians 2:2.
15. Heinrich Heine, *Letters on the French Stage*, trans. Charles Godfrey Leland (New York: Crosscup and Sterling, 1840), 255.